IMAGES OF LONDON

EALING

Greetings from
Ealing.

IMAGES OF LONDON

EALING

JOHN ROGERS AND REG EDEN

TEMPUS

Frontispiece: A multi-view card, published by Chaucer Postcard
Publishing Company, Herne Hill, 1903. It offers a fine
contemporary overview of the Borough of Ealing.

First published 2004

Tempus Publishing Limited
The Mill, Brimscombe Port,
Stroud, Gloucestershire, GL5 2QG
www.tempus-publishing.com

© John Rogers and Reg Eden, 2004

British Library Cataloguing in Publication Data.
A catalogue record for this book is available from the British Library.

ISBN 0 7524 3153 6

Typesetting and origination by Tempus Publishing Limited.
Printed in Great Britain by Midway Colour Print, Wiltshire.

Contents

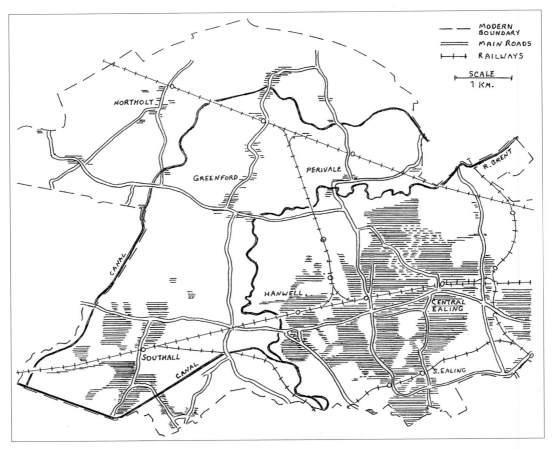

Ealing, 1920. The map shows the area covered by this book within the modern boundary of Ealing. The shading indicates the built-up areas in 1920, which explains why at weekends, as late as the 1930s, Londoners flocked to the genuine countryside so close to home for rambles and cycle rides around Perivale, Horsenden Hill, Greenford and Northolt.

Acknowledgements

Our thanks go to all the friendly people of Ealing who helped us with their memories, information and encouragement, but especially to Jonathan Oates and his helpful staff in the Local History Section at Ealing Central Library, to Ealing historian Paul Fitzmaurice for his advice and for loaning the five postcards in the book which do not belong to Reg Eden, and to the photographer Norbert Galea for his advice on the reproductive suitability of the postcards.

Introduction

This book is dedicated to the West London Postcard Club because, if the club did not exist, the book could not have been written. Reg Eden and I have been members since it started in 1989. When Tempus contacted the club to invite members to produce a book on a local area, I decided to act. Having written a number of books (including one as yet unpublished on rural walks around West London) I felt qualified; the problem was that I owned no topographical postcards, but I knew a man who did! Reg Eden has been collecting postcards of Ealing for 25 years. Together with his wife Eileen, he has been prominent in supporting the Friends of St Mary's Perivale, the beautiful former parish church. Reg is also a keen follower of John Betjeman and is busy compiling a glossary of Betjeman terms.

Most local history books based on postcards use material gathered together from several sources and archives. This one is different because, with the exception of just five cards, the 200 plus postcards and ephemera shown are all from Reg's unique collection. The book, therefore, does not claim to be a complete history of Ealing, but over 95 per cent of the pictures have not appeared in any previous publication so far as we know, and much important historical data has been dug out from obscure sources for the first time.

The emphasis is on the period 1900 to 1914, the golden age of picture postcards. The area covered is the whole of the modern borough of Ealing, including Southall, but excluding Acton. The eastern end of the borough is excluded because it is covered so thoroughly by Dr Jonathan Oates' book on Acton, published by Tempus in 2002.

Ealing comprises an amalgamation of parishes, each with a similar history. A group of cottages clustered around a church, more often than not called St Mary's, would grow into a small village whose centre was eventually some way away from the original hamlet. This certainly applies to Hanwell, Greenford, Perivale and Southall as well as to Ealing itself. Read on to see how Ealing, proud of its nickname 'Queen of the Suburbs', became an important Middlesex borough just over a century ago, and gradually absorbed the surrounding parishes and boroughs in a series of stages to form today's thriving and versatile London Borough of Ealing.

John Rogers

Overleaf top: Employers and employees at a timber mill, West Ealing, 1890s. The firm is believed to have been Boardman & Co.'s timber merchants and saw mills in Uxbridge Road.

Overleaf bottom left: Ealing's coat of arms, *c.* 1910. The device 'Respice, Prospice' translates as 'Look back, look forward'. The oak tree, which appeared on the arms of many boroughs, was a symbol of strength and longevity. It had no connection with Acton's oak, as the boroughs did not merge until 1965.

Overleaf bottom right: Nurses advertising Ealing's Tank Day, 13 March 1918. A procession, mayoral address and a real tank outside Ealing Town Hall raised the huge sum of £250,000 from the sale of War Bonds on the day.

EALING.

RESPICE PROSPICE

HERALDIC SERIES.

one

Looking South

South Ealing Underground station, 1914, looking north up South Ealing Road towards St Mary's church. The station was opened in 1883 to serve the District Line and immediately promoted development of the Ealing Park Estate nearby. The station was rebuilt in the 1930s to accommodate the extension of the Piccadilly Line.

This chapter, however, could easily be entitled 'Where it all began', because from the twelfth century the original hamlet of Ealing (albeit spelt variously 'Yelnge' or 'Xelling' etc.) was a group of buildings clustered around St Mary's church, with the even smaller hamlet of Little Ealing 1km further southwest, and Ealing Dean to the northwest.

It was another small collection of buildings to the north, called The Haven or Ealing's Haven in the eighteenth century, which eventually developed into the modern centre of Ealing. This came about first because The Haven lay on the Oxford (i.e. Uxbridge) Road and became a staging post for the stage-coaches, followed in 1838 by the building of Ealing Haven station (now Ealing Broadway) on the main GWR line.

Opposite: St Mary's church, in a postcard published by Louis Levy, *c.* 1900. The mid-Victorian building, dominated by its disproportionate tower, especially in this full-frontal view, has variously been described as elaborately ugly, early French Gothic style, eccentrically elephantine (Pevsner) or a Constantinopolitan basilica – take your pick!

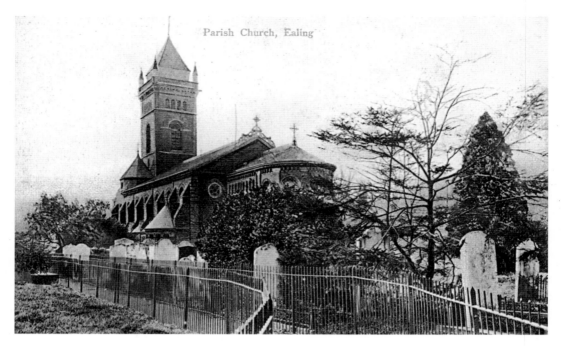

Parish Church, Ealing

St Mary's church, seen from Baillies Walk, showing that some of the Georgian building remains. The first church on this site was built before 1127, dedicated to St Mary in 1228, and lasted for 600 years, gradually deteriorating and finally collapsing in 1729. Services were held in a temporary wooden building nearby until sufficient funds could be raised for a more permanent solution. Building work commenced in 1735 and the new St Mary's, built in classical Georgian style, opened in 1740.

The church we see today is a re-modelled and enlarged version of its predecessor, designed by S.S. Teulon. Work commenced in 1865, the church was officially opened in 1872, and the building was completed in 1874. The basic proportions of the previous building were retained, but the roof was raised and the huge tower was completely new.

Further major improvements and refurbishments have been carried out in recent years, and the church was re-opened in June 2003 by the Bishop of London. 'Stonkingly wonderful' is how the Bishop of Willesden is reported to have described the improved church.

Baillies Walk is still a quiet footpath, half a kilometre long, heading east alongside allotments to Ascott Avenue. It was probably named after James Baillie who lived at Ealing Grove until his death in 1793. Ealing Grove was a mansion and large estate lying to the north further up St Mary's Road. The allotments were provided out of a charity established by Lady (later Dame) Jane Rawlinson in 1720. She also founded St Mary's Girls School and was buried in the churchyard. On the north side of Baillies Walk lay the original grounds of Great Ealing School before it moved in 1846 to 'The Owls' on the other side of St Mary's Road.

Above: The Rose and Crown, 1903. Standing behind St Mary's church, this was the first inn in the parish that travellers reached on the road from Brentford to Ealing. It was built on the site of a farm some time before 1823. The scene is unrecognizable today: only the pub name, the brewer and the wall on the left are unchanged. Even the chimneys have been re-built and moved, but the pub is still welcoming and popular.

Left: Ealing War Dressings Association, *c.* 1916. The Association was formed by a group of ladies who collected subscriptions to fund bandages which would be sent for wounded troops in France. Their headquarters, 2 Grange Road, was a private nursing home and hospital in a large house which no longer exists.

Lammas Park, *c.* 1900. In an age of innocence, children play a dancing game in the park. Their dresses indicate the Victorian era, in this early postcard issued by Misch & Co. in their Camera Graphs series. The distant houses are in Lammas Park Road. In 100 years only the trees have altered. In particular, the monkey puzzle tree (on the right) is now 12m high!

The origins of the park were not straightforward. The fields comprising the park were bought by the Local Board from six different landowners. The largest area of some seventeen acres (out of a total of twenty-five acres) was bought from the Ecclesiastical Commissioners for £1,775; this was the 'lammas' field which was sold 'subject to the lammas rights of ratepayers and all rights of common or past usage'. (Lammas meant the medieval right of manorial tenants to graze cattle and other animals on stubble after the harvest.) The park officially opened on 1 August 1883, that date appropriately being Lammas Day.

The problem for the Local Board was that the conditions imposed meant that livestock could still be grazed in the public park. In the first week of the park's opening, the Middlesex County Times reported that a Mr Godfrey was taking a walk when he was attacked by a cow. The problem continued for some years and a committee was formed to represent those with lammas rights.

Eventually in 1892, a declaration was sought from a Chancery court judge who determined that the Local Board could extinguish the lammas rights by paying a sum of £2,156 divided amongst the freeholders, copyholders and certain leaseholders in the parish. This was duly done and the park then became free of the lammas rights.

Opposite above: Lammas Park bandstand, 1904. Boys in mortar board caps and straw hats, probably from Great Ealing School, lounge in the park. St Mary's tower still dominates the horizon, but the bandstand is long gone.

Band Stand, Lammas Park, Ealing.

The Plough Inn, *c.* 1900. The inn, standing at the junction of Little Ealing Lane and Northfield Avenue, dated from the early eighteenth century. It was surrounded by three acres of pleasure grounds and bowling greens, and was reputed to have been a favourite haunt of Dick Turpin – no doubt handy for Hounslow Heath! The inn's quiet rural environment changed soon after this photograph was taken. In 1905 the Plough was completely rebuilt in an art nouveau style which it still retains today, and in 1909 modern development commenced, with houses and a row of shops being built on the pleasure grounds.

Above: The Convent of Nazareth, *c.* 1900. The grounds of Place House, built in the early seventeenth century, stretched over 500m from Windmill Lane (now Windmill Road) to South Ealing Road. It was rebuilt towards the end of the eighteenth century and renamed Ealing Park. After occupation by a succession of distinguished gentry, the estate was sold and broken up in 1882. Much of the ground became the Ealing Park Estate in 1886. The house and immediate surroundings became a convent occupied by the Sisters of Nazareth de Montlean. The postcard above (published by the Tourists Association, Turnham Green) dates from before 1903 when the house was passed to the Little Sisters of Charity.

Left: Miss Ethel Walker, 1908. One way for a minor professional entertainer to advertise herself in the Edwardian era was by publishing a postcard. Her address was an end-of-terrace house in one of the roads recently developed between Northfields station and Lammas Park. A telephone number on the card might well have improved her prospects.

The cast of St Anne's Convent High School play 'Zuricka', March 1938. The Little Sisters of Charity, founded in France by St Jeanne-Antide Thouret, set up the school in Ealing Park in 1903. It eventually closed in 1987. The house was then enlarged and refurbished, but it is Grade II listed, so the main facade today is still as shown opposite, 100 years ago. It is now the King Fahad (of Saudi Arabia) Academy for Girls.

Good Shepherd's Hall, 1928. The hall was built in 1905 in South Ealing Road on the corner of Temple Road. Its purpose was to act as a local mission church for St Mary's, catering for the expanding population in the southern part of its parish. From 1906 it had its own resident minister. It still exists but since 1978 functions as a church of the Assyrian Society of the United Kingdom.

Ealing Grammar School, 1906. Lady Byron founded a school at Ealing Grove in 1834. It had boarders, but took day boys for only 2d per week to attract children from working class families. Charles Atlee was headmaster from 1835 until it closed in 1852. In 1859 he started Byron House School in The Park. This was renamed Ealing Grammar School in 1896. By 1912 it had 200 boarders, but closed in 1917.

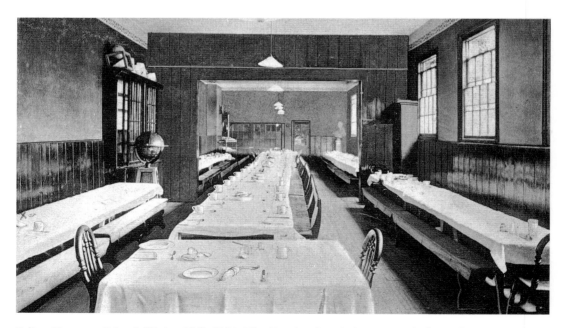

Ealing Grammar School, Dining Hall, 1906. The Tourists Association postcards shown here were issued to the boarders so that they could write home. The message on this card is from Master Sidney Turner. Retaining his original spelling, it went to an address in Lambath [sic]: 'My dear parents, I am very sorry I have to write and ask you weather you will send me some monney to pay for a large pain of frosted glass'.

Ealing Grammar School, Fifth Form, 1906. The message, from Master Stanley Blaze to his sister in Lincoln, gives an idea of the curriculum: 'Can you see me in this postcard ... but only half my head is seen. We have had scripture, grammar, Lady of the Lake, geometry practical, Euclid, dictation so far but I do not expect to get a prize...'.

Ealing Grammar School Chapel, 1906. After the school closed, part of the grounds became Ealing County Girls School, now incorporated in Thames Valley University. The school's iron chapel, however, still remains and is used by a private firm as an office. It stands in a private driveway off Kerrison Road, with an old petrol pump outside it. The chapel was used as an ARP warden's hut in the Second World War, and the pump provided an emergency supply for fire engines.

St Mary's Road, 1924, looking north towards Warwick Road. Frank Plummer had the chemist's shop at No. 33. J.A. Hipwood's placards stand outside his stationer's shop at No. 41, which is still a newsagent's today. On the extreme left is the Castle Inn, from 1832 the meeting place for Ealing's 'Court of Tenants', who made decisions about road improvements, street lighting and gas services, supported local National schools and later introduced electricity in the parish. The card was issued by R.W. Claridge, a stationer at No. 13 The Green.

St Mary's Road, 1909. This road connected the original village with the new centre of Ealing. Looking north from Disraeli Road towards the start of Ealing Green, the view surprisingly has not changed much. Out of shot, on the right, is the Red Lion pub which was to become a favourite 'local' for people working at Ealing Film Studios nearby.

two

Central Ealing

Above: Multi–view postcard, *c* 1930. This card captures well the mix of Ealing's central area that still holds true today, comparing the bustle of the Broadway with the peace and quiet of the parks and greens nearby.

This chapter is rightfully the biggest in the book, although the area covered is relatively small: the environs of Haven Green, The Mall, Broadway and New Broadway, High Street, Bond Street, Ealing Green, Walpole Park and Ealing Common. But what an area and what contrasts!

Although not a complete history, we will see how Haven Green developed, the considerable influence of Charles Jones, and the coming (and going, in some cases) of the churches. The remarkable story of Pitshanger Manor and Walpole Park is told with a sequence of postcards, and of how that great 'lung' near Ealing's heart might have been suffocated by housing.

The coming of the trams caused more rapid development than the first trains sixty-three years earlier and this applied particularly to the growth of the large shops and shopping parades. Anyone familiar with old Ealing Broadway will recognize this description from a postcard sent by a young lady to her friend in the early 1920s: 'Come and see us. I know you would like this place. The shops are fine ones .... and much the latest. There is a large church on the corner, big drapers on the other corner, also a big one opposite'.

And I have not even mentioned the stories behind Ealing Theatre, the Town Hall and the world's greatest tennis player! Read on...

Opposite below: Pitshanger Manor seen from Walpole Park in a Louis Levy (LL) postcard, *c.* 1910. The house has an illustrious history, regarding its builders, owners, residents and usage. The original house was owned by the Gurnells, a Quaker family with interests in trade and banking. It was enlarged in 1770 by the architect George Dance the Younger. John Soane acquired the house in 1800 for his own residence, and in 1802 rebuilt it, but retained the George Dance wing. In the 1840s it was bought by Spencer Walpole, who became Home Secretary. Walpole married Isabella (daughter of the former Prime Minister Spencer Perceval) and installed his wife's four unmarried sisters in Pitshanger Manor to live there for the rest of their lives.

"OH DRY THOSE TEARS."..
- WALPOLE PARK ----- EALING-

Above: An alarming encounter in Walpole Park, *c.* 1910. The grounds of Pitshanger Manor House encompass thirty acres of parkland right in the centre of Ealing.

7 EALING. — *Library Walpole Park.* — LL.

1 EALING. — *Public Library.* — LL.

The entrance to Walpole Park, *c.* 1903. Elegant Edwardian ladies, and a little girl with her dolly's pram, are coming away from the new free public library. The imposing Grade I listed gateway to Pitshanger Manor was designed by John Soane.

Above: The grand opening of Walpole Park, 1 May 1901. In the 1880s, Ealing's first District Surveyor Charles Jones (1830-1913) suggested to Sir Spencer Walpole that the grounds should be bought as a public park to save it from developers who even then were threatening to build on all the district's open spaces. Walpole died in 1898, but his son (also named Sir Spencer Walpole) abided by his father's wishes. In 1900, he sold the Manor and grounds to Ealing Council for £40,000. Middlesex County Council paid £10,000 towards the purchase.

But what should the park be called? Ealing Council initially chose Perceval Park, and Manor Park was also mooted. By the opening day, however, the final choice was Walpole Park. The park was then officially declared open by the Right Honourable Lord George Hamilton, Ealing's MP and Secretary of State for India.

These were auspicious times for Ealing. Just one month later, on 3 June 1901, it was incorporated as a borough, the first in the County of Middlesex.

Opposite above: Pitshanger Manor in another Louis Levy postcard, *c.* 1920. This gives a good view of three of the four statues with which John Soane embellished the entrance. Frederika Perceval was the last sister to die, aged 95, in 1900. Ealing Council then bought the house and grounds. The latter became Walpole Park, and from 1902 the Manor House housed Ealing Library. This lasted until 1984, when the library moved to the new Ealing Broadway Centre and the house became the Pitshanger Museum and Art Gallery.

Above: Ealing Technical Institute, 1906. Technical classes, held in the evenings for adults, commenced in Ealing as early as 1842. Art classes were added in the 1880s, with science starting in the 1890s. These were held in the Ealing Free Library for some years, but from 1901 to 1913 the building called The Hall was used for classes. That is the house shown above, which stood on Ealing Green close to Pitshanger Manor. It had been the home of Spencer Walpole, a Home Secretary and Chairman of the GWR Company, after whom Walpole Park was named.

Above: Empire Day, 1908. Walpole Park resounded to the strains of:

> *What is the meaning of Empire Day?*
> *Why do the cannons roar?*

On Monday 25 May 1908, 6,000 children from all the schools in Ealing gathered in the park for the annual celebration of Empire Day. The Middlesex County Times described it thus: 'Young Ealing had come in its thousands to hear of the glories and responsibilities of Empire, to be told of the magnitude of the inheritance in which it had a share'. Today, it sounds as remote as ancient Rome.

On the platform, the guest of honour was Sir John Alexander Cockburn KCMG, MD, late premier of South Australia. The mayor, G.C. Farr JP, then led all present in Rudyard Kipling's prayer, which was written on one of the banners:

> *Lord God of Hosts, be with us yet*
> *Lest we forget, lest we forget.*

Every one of the 6,000 children then received a gift from the mayor – a bag containing a bun, an orange, chocolate and some sweets. The postcard was posted a few days later by a young lady who was present, and she says 'What a glorious day; puzzle – find me!'.

Opposite below: Mattock Lane, 1910. Looking east from Culmington Road, only the trees have altered. The delivery cart belonged to Hornby's Hygienic Dairies, with branches in Argyle Road and Sandringham Parade.

The Aviary, Walpole Park, *c.* 1955. A park keeper shows off Cocky the white cockatoo to pupils from Ealing Grammar School for Boys. A retired council employee can just remember him: 'His name was Charlie Whitbread. The ETC on his cap stood for Ealing Town Council. It wasn't the official name of the borough, but they used to stamp it on any property that couldn't be nailed down, to stop it being pinched'.

The lake in Walpole Park, *c.* 1930. The lake was excavated in 1905, by gangs of twenty-five men, as part of the Council's attempt to alleviate the local unemployment problem. Its intended summer use was the sailing of model boats, as shown here; in winter they hoped it would make a skating rink.

Ealing War Memorial, 1939. Designed by Leonard Shuffrey and dedicated on 13 November 1921, the stone walls on each side of the gateway to Pitshanger Manor were completely filled with the names of Ealing's fallen in the First World War. After the Second World War, the walls were raised and extended to add the tragic list for that war. It seems poignant that this particular postcard was posted in June 1939 to an address in Belgium.

Ealing Green, *c.* 1903. Children play on the green, with Christ Church on the horizon. The scene had not always been so peaceful, however, as in earlier times it was the place where the Ealing Fair was held every June. It attracted people from far and wide, but it got too rough for local residents and was suppressed after 1880.

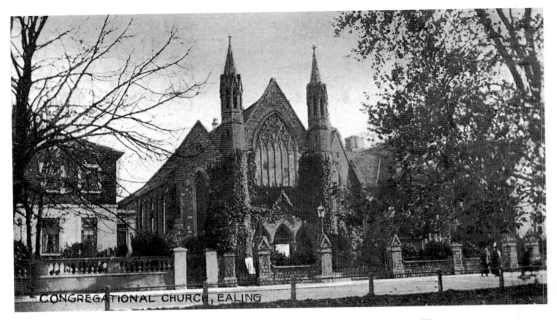

Ealing Congregational church, 1923. Dr John Owen, Vicar General to Cromwell's government, lived in a house on the east side of Ealing Green from around 1650 until his death in 1683. Ealing Congregational church was built on the site of that house in 1859-60. It was designed in Gothic style by Charles Jones and was the first of many fine buildings erected by him in Ealing. Since uniting with the Ealing Broadway Methodists in 1972, the name Ealing Green church has been adopted.

EALING CONGREGATIONAL CHURCH,
EALING GREEN, W.5
THE DEDICATION OF LITTLE CHURCH
and
THE NEW BUILDINGS
will take place from
Thursday, July 1st to Monday, July 5th.

Thursday,	7.30	Preparatory Quiet Hour. Rev. A. G. Matthews, M.A.
Friday,	8.0	Dedication Service.
Sunday,	11.0	Public Worship Rev. Malcolm Spencer, M.A.
	11.0	Little Church. Rev Wilton Rix, B.A.
	3.0	Sunday School Festival. Rev. Charter Piggott.
	6.30	Rev. Wilton Rix, B.A.
Monday,	8.0	Speaker : Rev. John A. Hutton, D.D.

Ealing Congregational church, invitation to a dedication, 1926. This postcard was sent out to announce the dedication services for a new 'little church'. This had been erected behind the main church and was intended for the specific use of children. The building still survives but is now leased to a play group.

High Street, The Green, 1920. That was the correct address of the parade of shops built in 1902. Bon Marché, outfitters, is just out of shot on the right. Then, after Hooper's ironmongers, comes John Snell bootmaker, Thomas Marns, a chemist advertising Idris mineral waters, Herbert Stones tobacconist and Fred Moore confectioner.

Bond Street, c. 1939. When Bond Street was created in 1905-06, cutting through the Ashton Estate, it provided an alternative to the High Street as a way into the Broadway from the south. Until the Ealing Broadway Centre was opened in 1985, Bond Street could claim to be Ealing's most recent shopping development.

High Street, Ealing, *c.* 1910. J.L. Taverner's, 'the cheapest drapery in Ealing', is prominent in the picture, with their greatest rival Eldred Sayers in the far distance. Not surprising, though, as this was an advertisement postcard published by Taverner's.

Wakefield's branch at No. 137 Brentford High Street, *c.* 1903. Frank Wakefield worked as a photographer in Ealing for over fifty years. He founded the firm which became the main photographic business in the area. The head office was at No. 1 Ealing High Street, and branches soon sprang up in West Ealing, Hanwell and Chiswick, as well as in Brentford. Frank was living at No. 49 Uxbridge Road when he died on 12 March 1929 aged 84, having taken no active part in the business for many years. Wakefields were a major publisher of local postcards, and forty-five of the illustrations in this book are taken from their publications.

The corner of Ealing Green and The Grove, 1905. The main turreted building, built 1902, remains unchanged externally despite recent internal refurbishment into luxury apartments. The inn sign left belongs to the Queen Victoria Hotel (originally known as the Horse and Groom) which lies out of the picture to the right of the fashionable Edwardian ladies. Its name changed, once again, in 1995 to Finnegan's Wake.

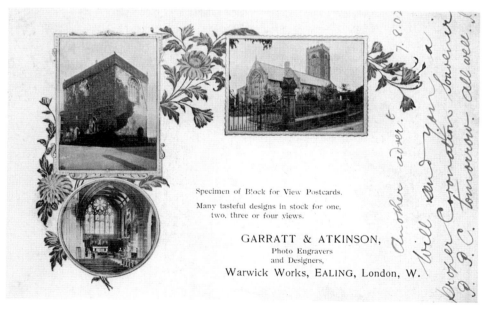

Specimen of Block for View Postcards.

Many tasteful designs in stock for one, two, three or four views.

GARRATT & ATKINSON,
Photo Engravers
and Designers,
Warwick Works, EALING, London, W.

Garratt & Atkinson advertisement postcard, 1902. They were one of the oldest established firms of engravers in this country. They started as Garratt & Walsh in Farringdon Street, London, and moved to Warwick Road, Ealing, in 1896. E.H. Atkinson was the photographer, and the firm published many of his local views as postcards.

Inspection parade of Ealing's Special Constables at Ealing Cricket Club ground, Corfton Road, Sunday 30 May 1915. There was a great shortage of special constables, recruited from men who were too old for active military service. They were needed to replace policemen who had enlisted.

St Peter's church, *c.* 1910. A small iron church in Mount Park Road soon became inadequate for the high class area to the north of Uxbridge Road. Mr J.D. Sedding commenced building St Peter's but he died in 1891, and his assistant Henry Wilson completed the task in 1893. With its yellow brick and boxed stone in decorated style, arts and crafts overtones, and a huge west window, it has been described as 'architecturally the most distinguished of Ealing's churches'. It took over part of the Christ Church parish in 1894.

Above: The Mall, 1903. The building on the left of this Louis Levy postcard was designed by Charles Jones and built in 1874 to be used as the offices of the Ealing Local Board. It served Ealing well until the Town Hall was opened in 1888. The building was then occupied by the London & County Bank, and much later by the National Westminster Bank.

The parade of shops on the right was built in 1902 on the site of old almshouses.

Right: Donald McGill postcard, *c.* 1910. McGill's saucy humour was all the rage in postcards at seaside resorts, but the respectable residents of the 'Queen of the Suburbs' probably did not take too kindly to being associated with it.

Ealing IS NO PLACE FOR A PARSONS SON

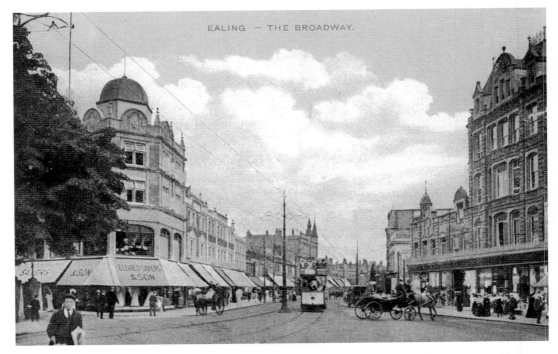

The great department stores, Ealing Broadway, 1907. The Eldred Sayers drapery business started in 1837 and prospered for over 100 years. Sayers' department store on the left, at the corner of Spring Bridge Road, was enlarged with a domed extension in 1902 after the arrival of trams had increased the number of shoppers. Sayers' business extended well beyond Ealing, with drapery and other goods being supplied to British families living in India.

Eventually Bentalls bought the site from Sayers in 1950. They stayed there until 1984. The original Sayers building on the corner was then demolished and the Waterglade Centre (later Arcadia) was erected on the site.

On the right stands the John Sanders store. John started his business by opening a single drapery shop in 1865, on the corner of Uxbridge Road and Lancaster Road. He was soon expanding into adjoining shops. By 1920 the Sanders shops occupied Nos 54-60 and 69-79 in Ealing Broadway. The rather uneven row of shops was rebuilt into a single facade in the period 1932-35.

On 3 July 1944 a V1 flying bomb (or doodlebug as we called them) scored a direct hit and completely demolished the whole western end of the store. Repairing the war damage did not commence until 1958 when the store was rebuilt minus the previous top storey. Rebuilding again took place when Marks & Spencer occupied the site in 1991.

Station Approach, Ealing Broadway.

Station Approach, Ealing Broadway, c. 1908. Foster's outfitters occupied the corner building on the left for several decades. On the first floor above them, Goodman's Teeth Institute(!) had a much briefer tenure. In the centre, by the policeman, the lamp standard is one of the original air-cooled transformers installed when Ealing first generated its own electricity in the late 1800s.

In the distance is the distinctive roof of the GWR station, with the offices of Jeayes Kasner, coal merchants and agents for GWR. To their right are Burley & Brackenbury, auctioneers, and the Feathers Hotel on the corner, which replaced an earlier inn of the same name in 1891.

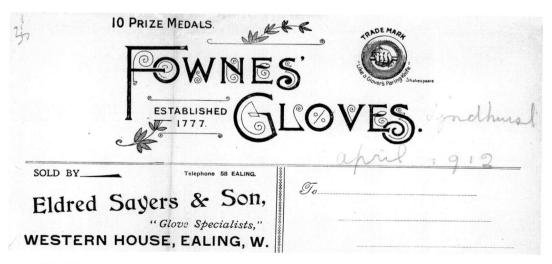

Eldred Sayers' glove envelope, 1912. Eldred Sayers did not simply sell gloves over the counter. They also packed and posted them in specially made envelopes.

Above: Ealing Broadway, 1908. The General bus, coming from Shepherd's Bush, advertises the Franco-British Exhibition there. (It does not mention White City, because that name had not yet been adopted for the exhibition site.) The event was a huge success, attracting 8 million visitors in the first six months.

The shops on the left include some familiar names. Beyond John Hoadleys drapers, Hieatt & Gregory grocers and Ashford & Davis watchmakers, comes W.H. Smith. Further on is the Singer Sewing Machine Company, then the Car (& General) Insurance Corp. and Ealing Hippodrome (which we will visit later in this chapter). Then comes Liptons the grocers before Frank Harman, gent's outfitter.

On the right are Greenhaighs, dyers and cleaners, Maynards the confectioners, and Castle Hill & Hanger Hill Dairy Farms' outlet, in the row of shops lying between two separate branches of John Sanders.

In the background lie the Feathers Hotel and the building that originally housed the offices of the Ealing Local Board. The pavements are thronged with shoppers displaying a fine array of Edwardian fashions, including a nurse on the extreme right.

Opposite below: An unexpectedly busy scene at the northwest corner of Haven Green, 1916. On the left, a wagon is being unloaded, a horse drinking at the trough pulls a cart for Brooklyn Model Laundry (who were based at the corner of Northcroft Road and Belsize Avenue) and an open top bus passes houses which have long since been replaced by blocks of flats. On the right are an unaccompanied milk float and a horse-drawn cab. The distant parade of shops lies north of the station.

Above: Bentalls store, *c.* 1960. A Bentalls van turns into Spring Bridge Road in front of their store, which advertises 'over fifty departments'. Having occupied the site for thirty-four years, Bentalls moved into the new Ealing Broadway Centre in 1985. In 2001 they were taken over by Fenwicks who then sold the store to Beales.

Eaton Rise, Ealing. No. 2008.

Above: Eaton Rise, *c.* 1930. In the 1860s, this was the first road to be developed to the immediate north of Haven Green. Whinney House School was established in Eaton Rise and in 1888 it was described thus: 'a desirable home for Indian and orphan children', where 'Indian' meant children of British parents who lived in India.

CASTLEBAR ROAD, EALING.

HAVEN GREEN, EALING.

Above: Haven Green, 1911. Just north of the main route from London to Uxbridge, Haven Green (or Ealing's Haven) was one of the original Ealing hamlets. In the early 1880s there was a cluster of houses around the green and a school where the novelist Edward Bulwer-Lytton was a pupil.

When the railway came through Ealing in 1837, it cut across Haven Green and landowners were compensated for the loss of their common rights. Even the opening of Ealing Haven station did not immediately lead to a rapid increase in housing. To the east there were orchards and a dairy. Two roads led out of Haven Green, Castlebar Hill northwest to Perivale, and Haven Lane going north towards Hanger Hill. Apart from Eaton Rise, the area to the north of the green was not developed until the 1880s. Following the Metropolitan Commons Act of 1866, Ealing Local Board purchased Haven Green together with other greens and commons, to preserve the open spaces.

The green itself used to be bare open grassland without any trees or paved paths across it. The first trees, many of which still survive, were all planted around 1880. In the postcard above, No. 155 in the 'C.A.P.' series, Haven Green Baptist church is seen in the background, and the toddler with the puppy is wearing an outrageously huge bonnet.

Opposite below: Tortoise Green, 1906. This was the charming local name for the small green where Carlton Road meets Castlebar Road. The latter was the old route from Haven Green to Greenford and Perivale. The cyclist and the nanny with the pram are actually in Carlton Road. Castlebar Road runs across the end of the street. Development of this area started in the 1860s, but it was not part of Henry de Bruno Austin's grand scheme for the Castle Hill Estate (see Chapter Four).

Passengers and porters await a train at Ealing Broadway, *c.* 1905. The GWR line from Paddington to Bristol was originally planned as early as 1825, but it was not authorized by Act of Parliament until 1835. Opposition to it in Ealing was overcome when the local vestry voted eleven to four in favour, and construction commenced with the appointment of Brunel, aged 27, as Chief Engineer.

Ealing Broadway District Line station, *c.* 1900. The District Line reached Ealing in 1879, when Ealing Broadway terminus opened alongside the GWR station. The District Line was electrified in 1905 and the station was rebuilt in 1910. The Central Line started operating in 1920, and space was found for its platforms between the District and GWR lines. Eventually all three were merged into one station with a shared entrance in 1964 and the old GWR station was demolished the following year, leaving only the frontage.

Haven Green Baptist church, 1906. The church was built 1880–81 in Castlebar Road close to Haven Green. It was designed by Wallis Chapman to hold a congregation of 500, and built by Thomas Nye who lived in Ealing Green. It has been described variously as 'a splendidly ugly Victorian pile' and as having 'an elegant French Gothic style'. In 1928, some internal structural changes were made, the organ renovated and a stained glass window added.

Haven Green shopping parade, 1905. The horse-drawn cabs await fares from Ealing Broadway station. The parade of shops, constructed in 1891, is still recognizable today. Walter Sanders was a fishmonger, then after the Aylesbury Dairy comes Frederick Candy the butcher, H. Evans' fancy draper and D.L. Lewis, chemist, whose name still exists above the shop! Next is Arthur Scott, an electrical engineer (surely an unusual trade in 1905), a confectioner, post office and watchmaker.

St Saviour's church, *c.* 1910. St Saviour's started as a mission church in 1881 to serve the lower-class housing behind the Broadway called 'New Town'. The permanent church, brick with stone dressings, was built in The Grove in 1897-98 and opened in 1899. The St Saviour's Clergy House was built nearby in 1909 and accommodated three clergymen. In 1916 the church obtained its own parish which was split away from that of Christ Church.

St Saviour's Pageant, November 1923. An annual bazaar and pageant was held in November every year to raise funds for the church. The show chosen for 1923 was Iolanthe, and here are the performers, with the fairies more 'dainty and little' than Gilbert intended! Unfortunately, even the parish gazette does not record the names of any performers. An excess of £880 was raised towards the organ fund.

ST. SAVIOUR'S
CHURCH, EALING.

Above: The nave of
St Saviour's church, *c.* 1910.
The mix of stone and
brickwork gave the interior a
striking and original
appearance. This all ended on
the tragic night of
16 November 1940, when
three incendiary bombs fell on
the church. The clergy and
wardens managed to save
portable items such as
vestments and sacred vessels,
but the building was almost
totally destroyed. The whole of
the interior was gutted except
for the baptistry and the
west end.

Left: St Saviour's font, 1923.
The church was not rebuilt
after the war. Its parish
rejoined with Christ Church
which thereafter was re-
dedicated. The name of
St Saviour's lives on, however,
in the infants' school, the
clergy house and St Saviour's
Mall in the Ealing Broadway
Centre.

Left: Christ Church, *c.* 1900. The erection of a major church near Haven Green was a sure sign that the centre of Ealing was moving away from St Mary's. Christ Church was built in Uxbridge Road in 1850-52, to a design by Sir Gilbert Scott. This was the first time that the parish of St Mary's had been subdivided. This is an early postcard, dating from a time before the trams reached Ealing in 1901.

Opposite below: Ealing Town Hall, 1910. In the 1880s it became apparent that Ealing needed a town hall. Edward Wood provided the land, and he also donated some money towards the project, together with Lord Rothschild and Sir Montague Nelson, Ealing's first mayor.

Charles Jones designed the buildings required. The plans were indeed extremely ambitious, but they were carried through successfully, and the complex of buildings included a public library, public baths, a fire station, stables and workshops. One of the pools in the baths was designed so that it could double as a gymnasium or badminton court.

Connected to the Town Hall was the Victoria Hall, modelled on a medieval baronial hall, intended to be the major room for official functions.

The Victoria Hall and Town Hall were officially opened together on 15 December 1888 by HRH Edward, Prince of Wales. The main buildings are still in use today, although naturally there have been some extensions and changes made over the years.

Right: The nave of Christ Church, *c.* 1910. The church was the gift of Miss Rosa Frances Lewis, a wealthy parishioner, in memory of her father 'Gentleman Lewis', a Liverpudlian actor who loved Ealing. The site had been provided by George Wood, a wealthy landowner whose family owned much of North Ealing.

The church was damaged in the Second World War, but fully restored 1946-52. It was then re-dedicated as the Church of Christ the Saviour when it absorbed the parish of the bombed St Saviour's church.

Victoria Hall. Ealing.

Above: Firemen and their appliances, Ealing Fire Station, Longfield Avenue, 1903. The fire station was built in 1888 as part of the town hall complex, proof of the growing importance of the borough. It was enlarged in 1900-01, but a new and better equipped station was opened in Uxbridge Road in 1933. The old building survives, but nowadays look through the large engine doors and you find people working in offices.

Above: Ealing Theatre, *c.* 1905. The ambitious Edward Delavante built the Lyric Opera House in 1880, and opened it in 1881, but his operatic scheme was a failure. The building became the Lyric Hall until it was demolished to make way for the (New) Ealing Theatre. Victoria Hall was used as the local theatre temporarily until Edwin Stephens' Ealing Theatre was opened on 23 December 1899 by Sir Montague Nelson. The first show was a lavish production of the pantomime Dick Whittington.

The Stephens brothers also owned Drayton Court Hotel, the Feathers and Eel Pie Island Hotel. Their new theatre was a grand affair, with three dance rooms (including the Montague Ballroom named after Sir Montague Nelson), two restaurants, lounges, licensed bars, tobacconist's shop and two billiard rooms.

In November 1905 Walter Gibbons secured the freehold and immediately converted the theatre into a music hall with two shows a night. It seems likely that it was Gibbons who started calling it the Hippodrome, in playbills and in front of the theatre, but the building continued to be listed officially as Ealing Theatre. The restaurant below ground became a bar for the pit and billiard rooms, while the upper restaurant turned into a branch of Lipton's. The Montague Room became the first cinema in the building.

The place was a fully fledged cinema from 1914, later called the Palladium. The pit bar was used as an air-raid shelter in the Second World War. The cinema finally closed in 1958 and was demolished. W.H. Smith's have occupied the site ever since.

Opposite below: New Broadway, 1904. The parade on the north side was built in 1902, partially on the site of Christ Church Vicarage. Young's China & Glass Warehouse moved in from across the road, but No. 11 remained vacant for a while. Arthur Tyer's jewellers were at No. 10, with the Ladies' Agency upstairs. Alex Ewing's Piano Warehouse was at No. 9, but in 1905 Ernest Squire took over and his piano and music shop remained there until 1987.

Above: Tram passing the Railway Hotel, Ealing Broadway, en route to Uxbridge, *c.* 1905. Horse-drawn trams started operating through Acton in 1876, and electric trams followed in the 1890s, but Ealing's local authorities opposed them in case they would attract too many people and lower the tone of the area. Montague Nelson and Charles Jones led the opposition until 1899 when they eventually bowed to the wishes of the public for cheap transport. Trams started operating through Ealing to Southall in 1901.

All Saints Church, Ealing Common

Above: All Saints' church, Ealing Common, *c.* 1910. Common land is ground that is, or should be, protected for eternity. Regrettably, this is not always the case, but Ealing Common in this sense has been a remarkable success. John Rocque's map, published in 1746, clearly showed the size and shape of Ealing Common. It has hardly changed in over 250 years. Even the strange little rectangle that stretches towards the station and the small triangle northeast of the intersection of the main roads were there in 1746. Only the position and width of some of the tracks across it have altered, and of course it was then surrounded by fields.

The one building shown in 1746 was Elm Grove, a fifteenth century estate in the southwest corner. In 1808, the most famous person to have lived in the area moved in – Spencer Perceval, who in 1809 became Prime Minister and in 1812 was the only person holding that office to be assassinated.

Elm Grove was demolished in 1894, when Leopold de Rothschild bought the land for re-development. Perceval's daughter Frederika, however, bequested that a church be erected in memory of her father. Rothschild agreed and the church was built close to the site of Elm Grove. Hence All Saints' church obtained its dedication because Spencer Perceval was born on All Saints' Day (1 November).

Opposite below: New Broadway, *c.* 1950. The familiar 65 bus leads two 607 trolleybuses and a Green Line coach past Christ Church, where scaffolding indicates that wartime bomb damage is still being repaired. The railings in the centre of the road guarded the stairs down to an underground toilet.

Station Parade, 1915. Ealing Common & West Acton station, as it was called until 1910, opened in 1879. It served the branch line from Turnham Green to Ealing Broadway. The shops are on the north side of Uxbridge Road opposite the station. Filby's hairdresser's is nearest the camera, then after the empty shop comes Clarke's fruiterers, James Taverner's post office, Tonkin the oilman, and the open-top bus has stopped outside Gapp's the grocer on the corner of Fordhook Avenue.

Lady cyclists on Ealing Common, early 1900s. Many hobbies and activities suddenly became very fashionable in the Edwardian era. Sending and collecting postcards was one popular and relatively inexpensive pastime. Outdoors, cycling was all the rage, even though fashionable decorum as yet made no allowances for such physical exercise.

St Matthew's church, 1904. A tram on Uxbridge Road passes the church in this Wakefield's 'Wyndham' series postcard. The first church near the common was a temporary iron structure built in 1872 in Grange Park. This quickly became too small, so St Matthew's was built in 1883–84 in North Common Road, to a design by Alfred Jowers, on land donated by Edward Wood.

'The Great Wonder', c. 1910. Billy Cleall stands outside his cottage, which was in the road called Ealing Common (now simply The Common) between Grange Park and St Marks Road. He named his house because it was a 'great wonder' that his old cottage remained amid the newly built affluent residences. Billy was the local odd-job man, which included beating carpets for people on the common, but he was listed in the commercial directory as Cleall & Son, firewood dealers.

The interior of St Matthew's church, *c.* 1910. The church, seating up to 1,000 people, has a beautiful interior, with stained glass of cathedral quality and a superb three-dimensional reredos depicting the Last Supper. Revd Henry Charles Douglass was the first vicar of the church, from 1884 to 1916, having previously served as minister at Grange Park 1876-84. Revd Douglass' daughter, Mrs Dorothea Lambert Chambers, is regarded as the world's greatest pre-First World War lady tennis player, winning seven Wimbledon Singles Championships between 1903 and 1914.

Children's Corner, 1910. This was not far from Billy Cleall's 'Great Wonder' cottage on the west side of the common, and he enjoyed organizing donkey rides for the local boys.

Riding down The Common, 1906. In this unlikely Christmas card, a horseman in immaculate riding habit is on the road called The Common which borders the west side of Ealing Common. The view north, from the junction with Grange Road, is distinctly recognizable today.

Uxbridge Road flooding, 15 June 1903. The stretch where Uxbridge Road crosses Ealing Common seems to have been vulnerable to flooding early in the twentieth century, entirely due to the flat terrain with no available run-off for the water. It does not seem to be stopping the tram, however, from proceeding on its way to Shepherd's Bush. The postcard was published by E.H. Atkinson.

Above: Trolleybuses on Uxbridge Road, in a 'Photochrom' card, 1955. Quiet and clean, the trolleybus is remembered with affection by many Londoners. The 607 ran through Ealing, from Shepherds Bush to Uxbridge, which is shown on the mile stone as another nine miles from Ealing Common. The first trolleybus through Ealing ran on 15 November 1936. The last one ran on 8 November 1960.

Left: Typical Edwardian comic postcard. Hopefully, anyone who studies this book will agree with the sentiments expressed on this card and be able to answer the question. It was not for nothing that Ealing was known as 'the Queen of the Suburbs'. The card was published by 'B.B.' in their London series and printed in Germany.

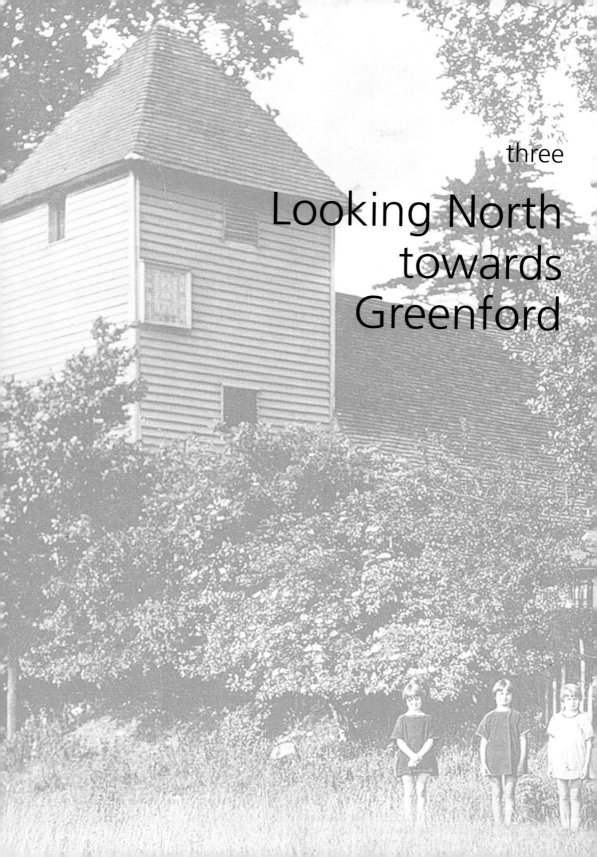

three

Looking North towards Greenford

THE POST OFFICE, PITSHANGER LANE

THE LYCH GATE, PERIVALE

SCOTCH COMMON

EALING

CASTLEBAR PARK

THE BRENT, PITSHANGER PARK

Above: Multi-view postcard, issued *c.* 1970 by an anonymous publisher. This card has some unusual features. It concentrates on the northern end of the borough, depicts Scotch Common which rarely features on postcards (with the best view in Ealing, of Horsenden Hill) and offers a shot of St Mary's lychgate uniquely looking away from the Perivale church instead of towards it.

This chapter covers the northern part of the modern borough of Ealing, from Hanger Lane in the east to the boundary with Hillingdon in the west. The area, approximately 7km long and 3km wide, encompasses a wonderfully varied landscape. It includes the pioneering Brentham Garden Suburb, a school which was considered the finest of all Ealing's excellent educational establishments, a famous haunted house, a church which is Ealing's oldest, prettiest and most historic, fine parks and woodland in the valley of the River Brent, and on top of Hanger Hill the site of the reservoirs which used to supply drinking water to the whole borough. North of the Grand Union Canal rises beautiful Horsenden Hill, truly an outlier of the Chilterns, and to the west we find Greenford and Northolt, both still delightfully semi–rural in places.

Two arterial roads, Western Avenue and Hanger Lane (in its guise as the North Circular Road) cut through the area like knives, bringing with them large industrial 'parks', but it is possible to move around and hardly notice them by careful choice of route. Even the industry has brought with it an Art Deco style of building much admired by some folk.

Opposite below: The orchard and rose walk, Princess Helena College, *c.* 1910. In 1935 the school moved to Temple Dinsley near Hitchin. Montpelier Primary School now stands on the site, with Helena Court on part of the grounds. The remaining space became an arboretum, now Montpelier Park.

Above: Princess Helena College, Montpelier Road, 1903. The Adult Orphans Institution was founded in Mornington Place by Sophia Williams in 1820, for orphaned daughters of military families and other gentry in straitened circumstances. It moved to Regents Park in 1824. King George IV and his sister Princess Augusta were patrons. Princess Helena (Princess Christian of Schleswig-Holstein, Queen Victoria's daughter) became president from 1868, giving her name to the school in 1879 before it moved to Ealing. The Prince of Wales officially opened the school in Ealing in 1882. When Princess Helena died in 1923, her daughter Princess Helena Victoria succeeded her as president.

The Princess Helena College, Ealing, A Corner of the Orchard and the Rose Walk

Princess Helena College, Ealing.

Above: The Main Hall, Princess Helena College, *c.* 1903. The school had a distinguished management team: Honorable Secretary Lady Jeune, Chairman Sir Joseph Savory Bart MP, Treasurer Lord Francis Hervey!

The Reservoir Ealing & Hillcrest Road W7

University College Hall, Ealing.

Above: University College Hall, Queens Walk, 1930. The building was originally called Castlebar Court and became a school during the Victorian era. It was then acquired by the University of London and altered to accommodate thirty-seven students and staff. On 17 November 1908 the Chancellor of the University of London, Lord Rosebery, performed the official opening of the new University College Hall. In the same year, the public could purchase shares in University College Hall Ltd. One of the points made strongly in the Hall's advertisements was that their athletic grounds were only fifteen minutes walk away at Perivale.

The building was used for other purposes during the two World Wars. In the First World War, it was turned into a convalescent home. Still called University College Hall in the Second World War, it became a school in 1940 for seventy-two Polish boys who had escaped from Poland to Paris and then fled to England. Soon after their arrival, the school was personally inspected by Madame Sikorski, the wife of the Polish Prime Minister in exile.

In the 1950s, the building reverted to its original name and became the Castlebar Court Training School for Nurses.

Opposite below: Fox's reservoir, Hillcrest Road, *c.* 1930. Two reservoirs were built on Hanger Hill to supply water to Ealing. The first and smaller one opened in 1882 on the south (far) side of the water tower. It has since been covered over. Fox's reservoir was opened in 1888 and named after Edwin G. Fox, Chairman of the Grand Junction Waterworks Company. It had a capacity of fifty million gallons, but was not needed when the Metropolitan Water Board took over, and was drained during the Second World War to prevent it being used as a navigational aid by enemy bombers. In 1972 it was filled in. The land is partly a sports field, but some of the area is preserved as meadows rich in wild flowers. The water tower remains as a protected building and a prominent landmark.

Above: Hanger Lane, 1901. This card, published by Boots Cash Chemists, shows a rural scene which only vanished completely in 1934 when the final stretch of the North Circular Road was opened from Harrow Road to Ealing Common. Even now, a pleasant woodland path still winds up the hill to the east. If you cannot completely escape from the traffic noise, at least you can avoid the fumes!

Above: Brentham Garden Suburb, *c.* 1912. Ebenezer Howard, founder of the garden city movement, thought people should be encouraged to improve their living conditions and formed a cooperative building firm in 1891. Six builders from the Ealing branch met in the Haven Arms and planned to buy plots of land in Woodfield Road on which to build some houses. Following the radical theories of William Morris and John Ruskin, they formed Ealing Tenants Ltd, with the encouragement and support of Henry Vivian, a Liberal MP. Prospective residents could buy shares which enabled the company to buy land and build the houses.

The company was registered in 1901 and Vivian Terrace had been built by the end of the year. The scheme was successful and fifty terraced houses had been built by 1905 in Woodfield Road, Crescent and Avenue, and Brunner Road. More land was bought, then Raymond Unwin and Barry Parker, the architects of Hampstead Garden Suburb, were brought in to plan better housing.

All houses were owned by Ealing Tenants Ltd and let at rents ranging from 6s 6d to 21s per week. Living conditions were a considerable improvement on other working class housing at the time. However, there was only one school, no church until 1916, and no local public transport until Brentham Halt opened in 1911 on the GWR Paddington-Northolt line.

The estate was completed by 1915. It was surrounded by open country initially, but this did not last. Ealing Tenants also started to sell some of the houses, but the village atmosphere has not changed and the estate is now protected as a conservation area. In 1969, the Brentham Society was formed to foster awareness of its history and preserve its character. The excellent book 'Brentham The Pioneer Garden Suburb' was published in 2001 to celebrate the centenary.

The postcard above, showing the Brentham Institute in Meadvale Road, was published by the Garden Cities and Town Planning Association, Grays Inn Place.

Opposite below: Ellerslie Tower, 16 Montpelier Road, *c.* 1930. In the 1900s, the West Middlesex branch of the women's suffrage movement held meetings here, hosted by Mrs Wallace-Dunlop. The house, however, became notorious as being haunted, with nineteen suicides and a murder reported to have occurred between 1887 and 1940. Some mysterious force was supposed to urge people to throw themselves from the tower. The building became uninhabitable and was demolished in 1970. Elgin Court now stands on the site.

Denison Road, Brentham Estate. This pre-First World War postcard had an interesting life. In 1917 it was sent via the Belgian Military Post, with a message written in Flemish by a young lady called Maria, to her father at 'E46 Depot' in France.

Denison Road, 1921. A later view of the road named after Frederick Denison Maurice, one of the people associated with the Brentham cooperative movement. A small open space on the left, at the end of the road, has recently been named Vivian Green in honour of Henry Vivian who pioneered the garden suburb. In Brentham's centenary year 2001, a plaque was unveiled by Vivian's daughter. It bears the legend 'Not "this house is mine" but "this estate is ours"'. The postcard was published by Kay's Post Office, Pitshanger Lane.

Brentham Institute, *c*. 1930. The founders of Brentham Estate considered that communal facilities were essential to provide educational, entertainment and recreational activities. It took ten years to achieve, but in 1911 the Brentham Institute was built in Meadvale Road and opened by the Duke and Duchess of Connaught. Sunday games were banned until 1922, and alcohol was not served until 1935. The Institute became a private sports club in 1947. It has produced some notable sporting personalities, including Fred Perry (tennis) and Mike Brearley (cricket).

Brentham Horticultural Society's outing, *c*. 1930. A keen interest in gardening was an integral part of life for many Brentham residents. So much so that four buses were needed in Denison Road to pick up all those interested in a horticultural trip.

A game of tennis on open ground near Woodfield Crescent, *c.* 1905. This was one of the first four roads to be built in the Brentham Estate. The first fifty houses in these roads were all terraced, to keep the costs as low as possible. A plaque which reads 'Ealing Tenants Limited 1904' can still be found on the facade of Nos 24 and 25 Woodfield Crescent.

PITSHANGER LANE AND POST OFFICE. EALING.   63267.

Kay's Post Office, Pitshanger Lane, 1969. Called Dog Kennel Lane originally, the track before 1901 merely led to Pitshanger Farm. In 1906 Ealing Tenants Ltd opened a cooperative shop in Pitshanger Lane but it failed. However, by 1909 a parade of shops had been established, run by estate tenants. It has been Brentham's local shopping centre ever since. N.B. Kay's Post Office published a postcard shown on page 64 in 1921, nearly fifty years earlier!

Ludlow Road, looking south, *c.* 1910. This street is typical of those in the Brentham Garden Suburb. It shows that moderately priced housing could be built in a variety of attractive styles. The lady in the Merry Widow hat has every justification for being proud of her local environment.

Pitshanger Park, *c.* 1920. The Brentham Estate was built south of the River Brent, leaving a space which was liable to flooding. The ground was used to establish Pitshanger Park, named after the farm which had been situated there. The park, covering 26 acres, still offers good facilities for tennis and bowls, a pleasant riverside walk and a footpath leading to St Mary's church in Perivale. The houses are in Meadvale Road.

View from Kent Gdns, Ealing.

Above: Kent Gardens, *c.* 1920. Sometimes old postcards present insoluble mysteries. This view, looking down Kent Gardens towards Harrow-on-the-Hill, clearly shows 'Castle Bar Works' inscribed on the wall right of centre. The sender writes 'I have marked a cross where the factory is that mother is in and where I go in with the pram'. However, it is a most unlikely spot for a factory and all attempts to discover its name or industry have failed.

Right: Unpaved country lane, Perivale, 1949. Could this be called a typical post-Second World War Perivale scene? Western Avenue had come, and with it came industrial estates, but parts of the parish were still rural even after the Second World War. In earlier centuries the population had actually dropped, down to twenty-eight in 1801, and had only risen to fifty-five in 1891. Strangely, there was no pub in the parish until the Myllet Arms was built on the site of Church Farm in 1936. (The Rector of St Mary's at the time suggested the name to commemorate the Myllet family.) Grange Farm survived until 1939.

Western Avenue, Ealing.

"KEEP THE HOME FIRES BURNING."

Above: Western Avenue and the Hoover building, 1935. Western Avenue was proposed in 1923 to provide work for the unemployed. Progress was slow and it was not until 1934 that construction started on the Greenford to Hillingdon stretch. In 1935 the cycle tracks had just been laid. Hoover's building, designed by Wallis, Gilbert & Partners as a prime example of Art Deco architecture, was built in 1932. Hoover's moved in a year later. A welfare block was erected west of the main building in 1937. Hoover's moved out in the early 1980s. Tesco bought the site and developed a superstore at the rear in 1992.

Left: 'Keep the home fires burning', 1916–17. One of a set of cards issued during the Second World War, each one showing a man in military uniform and a woman, usually a munitions worker. There were a number of munitions factories in Park Royal and some of the workers lived in Perivale. There is a local legend that Ivor Novello's patriotic song had its first public performance in Ealing. Sadly it is not true; it was first sung by Sybil Vane in a National Sunday League concert at the Alhambra Theatre, Leicester Square in the autumn of 1914, under its original title 'Till the boys come home'.

PERIVALE CHURCH, NEAR EALING

Above: The church of St Mary the Virgin, Perivale, 1924. Probably the smallest church in the old county of Middlesex, it was built in around 1135 of flint and rag rubble, and cement rendered with Reigate stone dressing. The nave roof dates from the second half of the fifteenth century, and the weather-boarded tower was added in 1510. The south porch was added in 1630, rebuilt in 1868 and altered again in 1911.

The sundial was added in 1818, but the one we see today is a replica. The weather vane was 'rescued' in 1850 by the churchwarden John Farthing when the old Market House in Brentford was demolished. It was replaced by a replica in 1985.

For many years, the church was thought to have had no dedication. In 1951, however, a copy of the fifteenth-century will of Isabella Miles of Perivale was found. This requested that she should be buried in St Mary of Little Greenford, that being the old name for Perivale.

The church closed in 1972 and was declared 'redundant', although it remains consecrated. In 1975-76 a group of volunteers led by Alan Gillett formed 'The Friends of St Mary's'. This developed into a registered charity and the building has become an arts centre serving the local community. There is a busy and wide-ranging programme of events – concerts, exhibitions, art workshops, etc. – and services are still held at times of Christian festivals.

Opposite below: St Mary's lychgate, 1914. Mrs Boosey (of Boosey and Hawkes, the music publishers) left a bequest in her will that one should be erected, and this came about in 1904. In this Wakefield's postcard, the Greenford U.D. Council notice on the right threatens prosecution for anyone even pushing a bicycle (or tricycle) along the path.

Above: The approach to St Mary's church, Perivale, 1895. If lychgates are usually very old, the one in Perivale is an exception. This early photograph, taken in the winter, provides a clear view of the church and old rectory before the lychgate was built.

Above: Interior of St Mary's, Perivale, 1893. The oldest item in the church is an octagonal font, dating from 1490. It was thought to have been lost, but was found in the tower in the nineteenth century under a pile of rubbish. The font cover is inscribed 'Gift of Simon Coston, 1665'. Several monuments in the church are dedicated to the Myllets, and brasses from 1500 depicting Henry Myllet and his family mark the entrance to the family tomb. There are also fifteenth century fragments of stained glass in the north chancel window.

The window in the south wall is dedicated to Nathaniel Ravenor of Ravenor House, Greenford. There are two fine memorials on the north wall. The one in view is for John Gurnell, 1745, attributed to Sir Henry Cheere (d.1781). The other monument (out of shot) is by Sir Richard Westmacott and is dedicated to Ellen Nicholas, daughter of Dr Nicholas, headmaster of Great Ealing School.

The best preserved relic in the church is the Early English arched doorway into the vestry, with remains of a holy water stoup. The doorway was the original entrance before the tower was built in 1510.

The photograph (not a postcard) shows the interior after the 1868 restoration by Robert Wiley, when major alterations included the installation of an organ chamber and new wooden pews. There were further alterations between 1907 and 1926, then a tower staircase and electric light were installed in 1930–32. Further restoration was carried out in 1968 by Laurence King, who designed the new Perivale church of St Mary with St Nicholas. After a period of closure and acts of vandalism, an enormous task was undertaken by the Friends of St Mary's to restore much of its former glory.

Opposite below: Canal bridge at Perivale, *c.* 1920. This narrow hump-backed bridge carries a lane from Perivale up around Horsenden Hill and is usually called Ballot Box bridge after the pub nearby. Although a popular route for hikers, it was dangerous for pedestrians and a separate footbridge has since been added.

West Ealing   Perivale Rectory

Above: St Mary's Rectory, *c.* 1905. This half-timbered building was built on the north side of the church in 1450, with the south wing added in 1699 and other later additions. John Farthing, churchwarden and local historian, lived there in the 1840s. Unfortunately it succumbed to dry rot and woodworm, and had to be pulled down in 1957.

Canal Bridge, Perivale.

Above: St Mary's churchyard, 1906. A search around the churchyard should reveal the graves of Dr Nicholas, headmaster of Great Ealing School; Robert Cromwell (d.1723) who was possibly related to Oliver, and George Elliot, the eldest son of General Elliot of Castlebar Park. You may also find the tomb of Thomas Bowler of Manor Farm, executed at Newgate after shooting and wounding a neighbouring farmer who had seduced his daughter.

The Boosey family had a vault there, as did the military Fitzmaurice family. Major General Fitzmaurice fought in the Peninsula Campaign and at Waterloo. He died at Drayton Green on Christmas Eve 1865, shortly after his son Captain Fitzmaurice had died in India.

The families mentioned were all local, but the churchyard also became a popular place for middle class Londoners to be buried in the eighteenth and nineteenth centuries; so much so that there was scarcely enough space left for parishoners. This led to legal action being taken against the rector to stop the burial of non-parishoners. The case was won and the practice ceased in 1906 when the above photograph was taken.

Unfortunately, in the 1970s when the church was neglected for a few years, the graves and statues in the churchyard were subjected to considerable vandalism and it no longer resembles the picture shown here. The only consolation is that its wild state makes it a haven for naturalists and birdwatchers.

Opposite below: Nursing facilities at the Park Royal Camp, 1924. These nurses might have been very busy, as there was an outbreak of smallpox in Harlesden that summer, but fortunately it was quickly contained. Bunty, who sent this card, had a more personal dilemma: 'I am staying 2 weeks instead of 1 because it is so lovely. I have made friends to a lovely girl – only she wears trousers and shirts'!

Above: Children's Camp Hostel, Park Royal, 1924. This temporary summer camp, which apparently had accommodation for 5,000 children, does not appear in the council archive records for either Ealing or Brent. It is possible that it was established to enable school parties from all over England to visit the British Empire Exhibition at nearby Wembley.

RIVER BRENT, STONEBRIDGE.

WILLESDEN

Two aspects of the River Brent

Above: Stonebridge, 1906. Just above the point where it reaches Ealing's modern boundary, the Brent glides through the bare, featureless fields of rural Middlesex. In John Betjeman's poem about the county, he addresses the river with the line:

> *Now what changes your waters show you.*

This seems particularly apt for the stretch where the Brent flows through the area known as Stonebridge Park.

Below: Brent Bridge, Greenford, *c.* 1930. The spot where Ruislip Road crosses the river is just as peaceful today, even though the busy Greenford Broadway is only 200 metres to the left. From here, heading south, the Brent River Park trail enters one of its finest stretches on its way to Hanwell.

1752   GREENFORD, RIVER BRENT

Oldfield Lane, *c*. 1905. This winding lane is, and always has been, at the heart of Greenford. Although no longer resembling the rural leafy track shown in the photo above, nor redolent of Betjeman's 'scent of mayfields', the southern section of Oldfield Lane is still a pleasant stretch in which to wander.

The lane linked the now vanished Greenford Green at its northern end with the hamlet clustered around Holy Cross church and, at its southern end, another group of cottages which is now Greenford Broadway. It now exists in two halves. Oldfield Lane North crosses the canal and the main railway line, ending at Western Avenue which cut through Greenford in 1934. Oldfield Lane South passes Holy Cross church, one of the few old buildings surviving, continues past Ravenor Park and ends beside the war memorial at the Broadway.

In 1924 the main Greenford Road was built, parallel to Oldfield Lane and bypassing Greenford, linking Harrow directly to the Uxbridge Road. This might have allowed Greenford to continue languishing as a sleepy backwater, as it had done for centuries, but this did not occur. North of Greenford station, the area was already developing as a thriving industrial estate. Further south, farmland was being developed into attractive residential estates.

Holy Cross church, 1907. The parish church of Greenford Magna was built in the twelfth century and much restored over the intervening years. It is situated close to the old manor house (which has not survived) 1km up Oldfield Lane from the modern Broadway. The postcard was published by H.E. Pearce, a wholesale stationer in Harlington.

A rapid increase in population between the wars necessitated a larger church to be situated next to the old one. Remarkably, the new church was constructed in the period 1939-42, when hardly any new civil building work was undertaken.

Holy Cross church interior, *c*. 1931, in a Wakefield's postcard. The church contains memorials to the local Ravenor and Coston families.

Greenford Trotting Track, *c.* 1925. In the 1920s, people would travel many miles to visit Greenford's most popular sporting venue. This opened in 1919 as the Greenford Driving Park, later better known as the Greenford Trotting Track. Primarily it featured the racing of two-wheeled carts drawn by ponies.

Run by the London Trotting Club Ltd, it claimed to have the widest cinder track in Great Britain, and to be the 'premier venue for this popular sport in the south of England'. However, fashions change; the popularity of trotting waned, greyhound and motorcycle racing was introduced, and the track finally closed in 1933. Jeymer Drive and Stanley Avenue were built on its site at the end of Birkbeck Avenue.

The postcard above features a photograph by K. Reitz showing ponies, minus carts, on the trotting track.

A trotting-pony, *c.* 1930. This animal, proudly shown at the Trotting Track, probably came from the Greenford Lodge stud farm, just before it was demolished to make way for Stanhope School.

Ravenor Park Estate

GREAT GREENFORD.

From Generation to Generation.

Head Office: ON THE ESTATE.
Telephone : Southall 253.

West End Office:
5, Market Place, Oxford Circus, W.
Telephone : 2831 Museum.

BANKS MAY BREAK, STOCKS AND SHARES MAY RISE AND FALL,
BUT FREEHOLD LAND REMAINS FOR EVER.

King & Hutchings, Ltd., Printers, 213, Uxbridge Road, West Ealing.

IT IS IN THIS BEAUTIFUL OLD-WORLD VILLAGE THAT WE
INVITE YOU TO MAKE YOUR HOME UNDER MODERN CONDITIONS.

Above: 'Beautiful Greenford', *c.* 1925. The Ravenors and the Costons were the two most influential families in Greenford for several centuries. Simon Ravenor, living at Ravenor House, became Constable of Greenford in 1596. Soon after 1835, however, the family left Ravenor House and sub-let the land to farmers. Early in the twentieth century, the farmland was sold to a Hanwell developer, and plans were made for a large residential estate.

Greenford Gardens and Ravenor Park Road were laid out by 1912, but the war interrupted development. Building resumed slowly through the 1920s and '30s, but in a haphazard fashion as several different builders were used because buyers of plots were encouraged to 'build their own house'. By 1926 the council had established name plates for roads and house numbers.

Coston Farm was bought by Ealing Council in 1928 to create Ravenor Park. Ravenor House was demolished in 1936.

The multi-view illustration above is a reduced copy of a page from a remarkably 'hard sell' brochure issued by Ravenor Park Estate Ltd in the 1920s. It was a compilation of new photographs and existing postcards.

Opposite: Ravenor Park Estate brochure, 1924. This developer's brochure tempted freeholders thus: 'Woodland Dells, steep, rising Grassy Slopes and Woody Hill-tops, can be seen for miles around. The District is one of the healthiest around London, and the Death Rate the lowest'.

King George V and Queen Mary visiting the Ravenor Park Estate, 1912. The royal car passes Ravenor Park Road, the first one to be laid out.

Oldfield Lane, near Holy Cross church, 1930. Several farms still functioned in the area and cows were herded through the streets. The building on the right, with the prominent clock tower, is the old village school. It still survives as the Edward Betham Church of England Primary School.

The village hall (left) was a redundant army hut after the First World War. Locals, with help from the Rockware Glass Company, formed the Greenford Village Hall Company, sold shares at £1 each, and raised enough money to convert the hut into a village hall. When this photograph was taken, it was doubling as the local library pending the opening of the new permanent Greenford Library in 1934. The village hall was pulled down in 1938 to make way for a second school.

Aberdeen Cottages and the White Hart, 1907. The cottages (left) stood at the southern end of Oldfield Lane, but were demolished before the Second World War. A small theatre, Greenford Hall, was built in 1966 just behind their site. The furthest building on the left was the White Hart Inn. It opened as a beer shop in 1845, but had closed by 1912.

Greenford War Memorial, *c.* 1959. The memorial, at the junction of Oldfield Lane and Greenford Broadway, was unvailed in 1921. It is inscribed:

> *Ye who live on mid English pastures green,*
> *Remember us and think what might have been.*

Surprisingly, it stands on the same stretch of green as shown in the picture above, but fifty years later.

Greenford Broadway, *c*. 1950, on a greetings card published by Overland Views, Uxbridge. The Broadway developed on Ruislip Road, the original east-west route through Greenford, despite being relatively remote from the railway, Underground and canal, and indeed some way from the parish church and the village school.

The Red Lion, Greenford, 1930s. The old Red Lion had stood at the junction of Windmill Lane and Ruislip Road (i.e. Greenford Broadway) since around 1726. In the early 1930s a new Red Lion pub, in mock Tudor style, was built on the corner of Greenford Road and Ruislip Road. At the time this photo was taken, the old pub was still standing and can be seen in the background with its prominent tall chimneys.

River Brent, 1950. Looking upstream from Greenford Bridge, this view has not changed much over the years. The road on the left is Costons Lane, providing a local reminder of the Costons, one of Greenford's great families who have lived in the area since the early seventeenth century.

The old Ballot Box Hotel, Horsenden Hill, 1907. This hostelry started as a beer shop in 1726 (or earlier) and became a pub in 1860. Nobody knows how it derived its unusual name, but in the past public houses were often used for auctions, inquests and electoral activities. In the 1930s the pub was moved north a little way along Horsenden Lane, to comply with the council's arrangements to make the hillside an open space for public use.

The Tea Gardens, Ballot Box Hotel, 1907. Pubs were a popular subject for postcard pictures, but their interiors and gardens appeared less often. This card and the one below may indicate the popularity of Horsenden Hill for day trippers and hikers. The Ballot Box was handily placed at Brabsden Green, on the slopes of the hill, with no other pub nearby. Its visiting clientele no doubt bought postcards as souvenirs of their outing or hike. The seating available shows the pub expected large crowds to come and sample the Benskin fine ales advertised above its roof.

Another view of the Tea Gardens, 1907. Again a young lady sits alone. Hopefully she has not been 'stood up'. All three Ballot Box postcards were issued by Wakefield's.

The view towards Ealing from Horsenden Hill, *c.* 1910. In this Wakefield's postcard, the water tower at Fox's Reservoir is prominent on the horizon to the left. To its right, beyond the fields, lies the relatively new Brentham Garden Estate. The GWR line crosses the fields on its embankment. Much closer is a brief glimpse of the canal and Horsenden Farm. As yet there is no Western Avenue and no Perivale Industrial Park between the railway and canal.

The Drive, Horsenden Hill, 1913. The hill's summit, at 83m above sea level, is the highest point in Ealing, and presents a steep climb of 55m from the Grand Union Canal. Its wooded slopes are the nearest we have to genuine countryside. Fortunately it was still largely undeveloped in the 1930s when the council acquired the hill for public use, despite local objections about 'undesirable day trippers' being attracted to the area.

The footpath from Greenford, 1912. A local resident, John Cordon, recalls his boyhood days in the 1930s: 'Our favourite hike was to Horsenden Hill. This was a long walk for little legs if you came from Greenford or Northolt. As I remember, we had to go up a long cinder path from the Greenford Road until we reached the Rockware Glassworks which made a heck of a clanking noise and belched out flames and fumes. Then there was a little concrete bridge over the canal. From thereon you could be way out in the country. And so we would make for the summit and arrive exhausted. Even jam sandwiches and tizer tasted good after that lot'.

The upper slopes of Horsenden Hill. This jolly picnic scene appears in a postcard sent in June 1918, but the photograph probably dates back to halcyon days before the First World War.

Northolt parish church, *c.* 1930. West of Greenford, across the canal, the little parish church of St Mary the Virgin stands proudly on its hillcrest. A religious building has probably stood on this site since the seventh century. A priest existed in 1086, and a building is recorded in 1140. Parts of the existing church are fourteenth century, including the font. From the thirteenth to nineteenth centuries, many Bishops of London were Rectors of Northolt, though they rarely visited this remote spot. Since 1864, however, patronage has belonged to Brasenose College, Oxford, who have appointed vicars ever since.

Willow Tree Cottages, *c.* 1930. Standing close to Northolt Green, four cottages were built around 1835 and housed farm workers from Court Farm. Believed to be the oldest surviving secular buildings in Northolt, two still exist, although only as empty dilapidated shells in the Rest Garden below the churchyard.

Northolt Post Office, 1908. The shop was run by M. Hinge, who also published local view postcards. (Was the postmaster perhaps any relation to Sarah Hinge, Greenford's lady blacksmith in 1841?) The post office is on the left; to the right, Willow Tree Cottages are almost hidden, the old school is on the extreme right, and St Mary's church lies behind.

The Church & Schools, Northolt

Northolt National School, 1907. This is one of M. Hinge's postcards (see above). It shows the school on the left, built in 1868 but in its last year before a new larger primary school was opened nearby to provide for the increasing population.

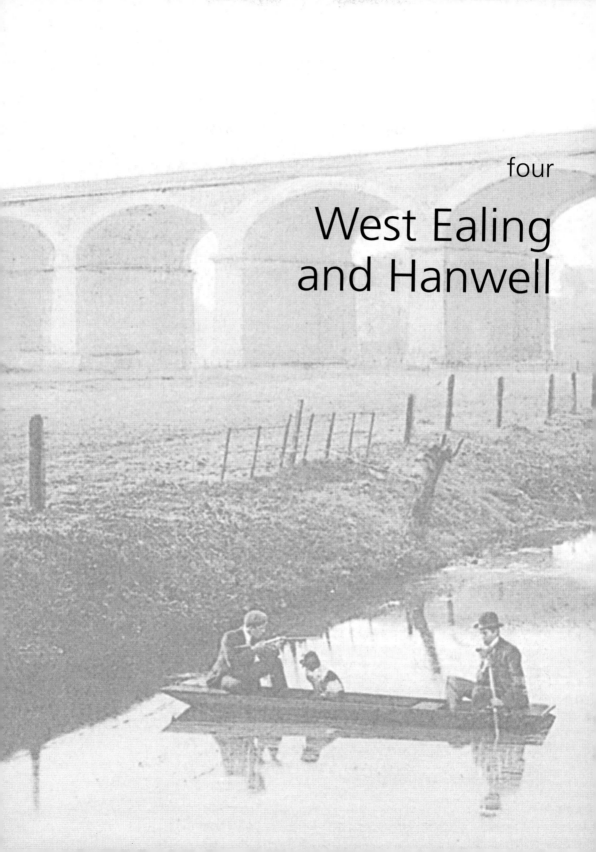

four

West Ealing
and Hanwell

EALING.

Above: West Ealing Broadway, 1907. What is, or was, West Ealing exactly? It lies around the Broadway (Uxbridge Road), Drayton Green Road and The Avenue. To the south lies Northfields, an early twentieth century residential development around Northfield Avenue (originally North Field Lane). For the purposes of this chapter, the area up to Castlebar Hill has also been included.

West Ealing was originally a hamlet called Ealing Dean, with inns clustered around a toll gate on Uxbridge Road. West Ealing station (originally called Castle Hill Halt) opened in 1871. Then the district around Drayton Green Road and the station became an area of densely packed working class houses, with many of the residents working for the Great Western Railway. It came to be known as Stevens Town, named after Stevens the landlord. At one census, 8,000 people were found to be housed in 700 dwellings, and it is significant that, in the 1880s, the district's only pawnbroker was situated in West Ealing. The status of the area remained virtually unchanged until re-development in the 1960s.

In the Wakefield's postcard above, a tram on Uxbridge Road approaches the junction with Drayton Green Road, where an Ushers' dray is delivering Wiltshire Ales.

Opposite below: Northfield Avenue, looking towards Mayfield Avenue, 1925. From left to right: John Hobbs' tailors, Mrs Stevens' stationers, John Brown the bootmaker, then the policeman is keeping a watchful eye on the Westminster Bank. Next comes Ernest Pickard the grocer, Leonard Woollard's ham and beef shop and Wickenden's funeral parlour.

Above: Trent Avenue, looking towards Windermere Road, 1910. This area had only recently been developed. Walter Morris's greengrocer's shop at No. 4 is on the left of the picture. This is very close to South Ealing station, but at the time was regarded as West Ealing.

Bradford's Jersey Farm Dairies at your service, c. 1915. Alfred William Bradford's dairy flourished for a few years between 1910 and 1918. Situated at No. 138 Northfield Avenue at the junction with Altenburg Avenue, it covered a wide area with its six milk floats. The shop was on the corner, and the dairy was in the gabled building behind it.

The interior of Bradford's Hygienic Dairy, c. 1915. The firm had a large number of employees and was efficient and prosperous. By 1918 Alfred Bradford, a highly successful entrepreneur, had sold the business to Long & Pocock and moved on to new enterprises. This postcard and the one above were the official Bradford Dairy cards provided to customers so they could order milk, butter and eggs. Alfred appears in both pictures, relatively young but clearly in charge. He later became an Ealing mayor and Freeman, Chairman of Brentford Football Club, and a Justice of the Peace.

The Green Man, *c*.1912. The inn, left of centre, dated from the eighteenth century when it stood near the toll gate on the Uxbridge Road. It was eventually demolished in 1981, to be superseded by a branch of W.H. Smith. This postcard is yet another to be published by a small local firm, this time C.E. Taylor, a West Ealing picture frame maker.

Note the posts in the middle of the road supporting the tram wires. Soon after the First World War these were replaced by stands on both sides of the road.

Looking east along Uxbridge Road, *c*. 1914. In the distance, the large white building on the right was the new Kinema cinema, built on the site of Ealing Cottage Hospital which was replaced in 1911 by King Edward Memorial Hospital in Mattock Lane. Renamed the Lido in 1928, the cinema has been used for a variety of entertainment purposes, but is now scheduled for demolition.

St. John's Church
WEST EALING

Destroyed by Fire Nov. 8th, 1920
10.30 P.M.

All Photos by WAKEFIELDS
No. 90.   EALING, W. 5   (Copyright)

BEFORE THE FIRE.

NEW (TEMPORARY) CHURCH, WEST EALING.

SOME OF THE RUINS.

AFTER THE FIRE.

ONLY BARE WALLS REMAIN.

St John's church, 1921. The first church for the expanding population of West Ealing was a temporary corrugated iron building near Green Man Lane in 1865. A year later, this was replaced by a wooden building which was moved from the grounds of St Mary's Vicarage to a site close to the western end of Mattock Lane. This in turn was replaced by a permanent church, on the same site, which was designed by E.H. Horne and consecrated in 1876.

Unfortunately, the French Gothic style building was gutted by fire on 8 November 1920. It was under-insured, but public subscriptions and fundraising efforts ensured that the church could be rebuilt.

St John's church rebuilt, c. 1950. The church was re-dedicated on 28 April 1923. This Photochrom postcard shows that the short spire of the original building was replaced by a battlemented tower.

The Avenue, 1904. The parade of shops at the southern end of the road presented a lively scene, with ladies on both sides of the road dressed in high Edwardian fashion. On the left is a builder's cart with ladders, while in the centre a covered wagon is being unloaded. In the distance, at the end of the road, towers the spire of St Stephen's church.

The Avenue, 1914. Two horse-drawn Hackney carriages wait near the cabbies' hut outside Drayton Court Hotel. This card can be dated to the First World War period, with a soldier bottom left passing W.H. Read's, the house agents, and the back of the postcard proudly proclaiming that it is 'Entirely British Manufacture'. Drayton Court still exists as a large busy pub with its own small theatre.

Above: Castle Hill School at No. 83 The Avenue, 1905. The school existed from 1885 (or earlier) until 1939. Cecil Lewis, its headmaster for many years, then continued to live there as a private tutor while his wife turned it into the Margam Guest House. Since 1957, however, it has reverted to full educational use with Ealing College Upper School occupying the building.

Left: Quex Products, *c.* 1939. Miss H.M. Lush ran an enterprising business from her own home for a number of years. This is a postcard she published to advertise her wares and which could be used by customers to place orders. The telephone number is of interest; St Leonard's Road is a turning off Uxbridge Road in West Ealing, but the area was covered by the Perivale exchange.

Opposite below: The Grange, St Stephen's Road, *c.* 1910. This house was built in 1891 on the site of the seventeenth-century mansion Castlebar Park. St Stephen's church fetes were held in its grounds for many years until the house was demolished in 1963.

St. Stephen's Church, Ealing.

Above: St Stephen's church, 1907. In the 1860s, Henry de Bruno Austin attempted to develop the Castle Hill Estate, from Scotch Common south to the railway line, but by 1872 he was bankrupt. His estate did get built, albeit considerably modified, but with St Stephen's church its focal point as he intended.

The church, viewed here from St Stephen's Avenue, was built in 1876, designed by J. Ashdown in ragstone, costing £6,000. The tower and spire were added in 1888-91 by Sir Arthur Blomfield. The building became unsafe and closed for worship in 1979. It was converted into flats in 1985, but its external facade is unchanged. Services have been held in the brick church nearby since 1986 when its foundation stone was laid by the Bishop of Willesden.

Above: Aerial view of Hanwell Broadway and St Ann's School, looking north up Boston Road. This postcard was published in the 1930s by Surrey Flying Services at the Air Port of London, Croydon.

Pause a moment and consider what immediately comes to mind if somebody mentions Hanwell. Older generations may instantly think of the Asylum, which is doubly unfair because the name was changed to St Bernard's Hospital back in 1937, and anyway it was situated in the parish of Norwood, not Hanwell!

Boating people will picture the impressive flight of locks on the Grand Union Canal, while to road users Hanwell is a small but busy Broadway on the Uxbridge Road. Educationalists will recall the Cuckoo Schools, while film buffs triumphantly recount a connection with Charlie Chaplin. Railway enthusiasts will naturally prefer to concentrate on Brunel and his viaduct. But I like to think of the historic church nobly set above the steep banks of the River Brent, or the excellent Animal Centre nearby (known locally as the Bunny Park), a small zoo which has been steadfastly ignored by postcard publishers over the years. So it seems there is something in Hanwell for almost everybody.

Opposite below: Hanwell Broadway, viewed from Vaux's store, 1905. On the right stands the Duke of York, an early nineteenth-century pub, the Clock House (W. Parson, jeweller), Rippons the chemist, and the London & South Western Bank (later Barclays). A Gapp's horse-drawn cart is delivering groceries.

Late shopping on Saturday night was a local tradition in the Broadway, with the Salvation Army Band serenading the customers, and shops staying open until midnight.

Above: Vaux's drapery store, Hanwell Broadway, *c.*1905. The building dominates the broadway, as it had done since early in the nineteenth century. This is one of many local view cards published by Vaux to promote their business.

Is the driver of the horse-drawn cart aware that there are trams about? The London United Tramways route from Shepherds Bush reached Hanwell in 1901.

Cuckoo Schools.　　　　　　　　　*Hanwell.*

Above: The Central London District Schools, 1905. The schools were built in 1856–57 to house poor children from Southwark and the City of London under the Poor Law regulations. The institute was known locally as Cuckoo Schools because it was built on part of the Cuckoo Farm Estate. It held over 1,000 children, including Charlie Chaplin who went there, aged 7, in 1896 and stayed for two years.

CENTRAL LONDON DISTRICT SCHOOLS　HANWELL W.7.　136

Above: St Mary's, Hanwell parish church, and Churchfields Recreation Ground, 1906. Some sort of religious building has stood on this site since the tenth century, but the present church dates from 1842, replacing the 1782 building which had become too small. Constructed of flint, brick and stone, it was one of Sir Gilbert Scott's earliest designs, in association with W.B. Moffatt.

The list of Rectors includes some interesting people: Dr Samuel Glasse 1781-85, chaplain to King George III; George Glasse, Samuel's son, 1785-1809; Derwent Coleridge, son of the poet, and more recently, Frederick Thomas Secombe, brother of Harry!

Some other familiar names are associated with the church. The artist William Yeames, who painted 'When did you last see your father?', was responsible for the frescoes in the chancel. Jonas Hanway (1712-86) is buried in the crypt; a friend of the Glasse family, he was a social reformer, founded the Marine Society, and introduced the umbrella to England. Two daughters of Gainsbrough lie in the churchyard, but their gravestones are difficult to locate.

The open hillside which drops down from the church to the River Brent is Churchfields Recreation Ground. It covers twenty-two acres and has been preserved for public use since it was bought by the council in 1898.

Opposite below: The CLDS's administration block, *c.* 1910. When the Poor Law was abolished in 1929, the Cuckoo Schools were transferred to London County Council who closed them in 1933. The land was sold for housing development, but the administration block was retained and became the Hanwell Community Centre. The clock tower, added in 1880, is still visible from some distance.

Above: River Brent at Hanwell, where it flows under the Uxbridge Road, *c.* 1910.

Opposite: Children playing on Boles Bridge, *c.* 1914. The footbridge has since been re-built, but it still carries the path from Dormer's Wells to St Mary's church, Hanwell, just visible on its knoll behind the trees.

Below: The confluence of the River Brent with the Grand Union Canal, *c.* 1910. This unusual 'season's greetings' card, published by Vaux of Hanwell, shows the canal with the river flowing in from the left under the elaborate footbridge.

Brent Bridge, *c.* 1908. A bridge has crossed the River Brent at Hanwell since the fourteenth century or earlier. It has been rebuilt or improved several times. Here a tram heading for Shepherd's Bush crosses the bridge in the period after 1906 when it had been rebuilt once again to facilitate trams more readily.

Greenford Avenue. The shops at its southern end look quite busy: from right to left, John Shepard's tobacconist, Evan Davis the oilman, Stanley Purkiss' fishmonger and greengrocer on each side of Enoch Clark's bakery, and on the corner of Shakespeare Road stands W. Walsham's post office where he also practised as a pharmacist and optician! Purkiss' handcart stands in the road. The year is 1914–15, with a newspaper placard proclaiming 'Cup Final not to be played at Crystal Palace' (because the Army had commandeered the ground).

A 14XX Class engine at Drayton Green Halt, *c.* 1950. This station is on the Greenford Loop line, linking Ealing Broadway to Greenford. The line started operating in 1903 and the halt opened a year or so later, encouraging housing development on both sides of the railway. 14XX and 54XX steam engines were replaced by diesel engines at the end of the 1950s.

Wharncliffe Viaduct, *c.* 1902. At 260m long and 20m high, the viaduct carries the main line from Paddington (Great Western Railway) over the River Brent at Hanwell. Built in 1835-38, it was the first of Brunel's major constructions. It was named after the Chairman of the Parliamentary Committee on the GWR Bill, Lord Wharncliffe, whose coat of arms is carried on the side of the viaduct. Queen Victoria used to halt the royal train on the viaduct so she could admire the view of St Mary's church on the far side of the railway.

The Iron Bridge, *c.* 1912. At the western end of Wharncliffe Viaduct, Brunel's bridge carries the GWR over Uxbridge Road. The original cast iron construction partially collapsed in 1839, and again in 1847. A wrought iron bridge was then built, and it substantially still exists. A distant tram is just visible in this Wakefield's postcard.

Greenford Hotel, *c.* 1950. Licensed premises for a site beside the Iron Bridge were first proposed in 1930, supported by the Iron Bridge Garage and the AEC Works nearby. The West Middlesex Golf Club and White Hart, Greenford, opposed and the licence was refused. By 1933, however, Greenford Hotel had been built. In 1974, it was bought and converted with new club premises but since the 1990s it is just another branch of McDonald's. (N.B. Sticklers for parish boundaries will say this page belongs under Southall. If so, please treat it as such!)

five

Southall

Above: People unfamiliar with Southall, or those who only know it by unfounded reputation, may be surprised by an investigation of the district. This is especially so when they ask if there is any connection between bustling Southall and sleepy Norwood Green, and is there anything in Southall worth writing about? The answer to both questions is, of course, 'Yes'!

The first surprise is that Norwood pre-dates Southall and, in Saxon times, was the more important manor. But nothing much ever developed at Norwood, whereas Southall grew in significant steps: in 1698 King William III granted a royal charter to Southall Market which still thrives today, the Grand Junction (later Union) Canal arrived in 1796, Southall station quickly became an important local junction after it opened in 1839, and the gasworks started operating in 1868. Southall may not have become any prettier, but it grew rapidly in size and importance while Norwood slept. The Southall-Norwood Urban District Council was formed in 1894, although the only direct link on the ground was, and still is, one bridge over the canal.

Today, Southall is in the forefront of the multi-national and multi-ethnic society of modern Britain, but its churches and manor house remain, hardly changed, among mosques and numerous Sikh and Hindu temples.

The postcard above, published around 1910 in the 'Gazette' series by John King, a Southall printer, appropriately shows the railways, the canal and a quiet corner of Norwood Green.

Opposite below: Southall War Memorial, 1925. Of the 3,500 men from Southall serving in the First World War, 800 did not come back. The war memorial, in front of the manor house, was deliberately modelled on the Whitehall Cenotaph.

OLD MANOR HOUSE & GROUNDS, SOUTHALL

Above: Southall Manor House, 1928. The house was built in 1587 for Richard Awsiter, whose family owned it until 1821. From 1879-95 it was the residence of William Frederick Thomas, a sewing machine manufacturer, generous local benefactor, President of Southall Cottage Gardens Association, and Norwood's first County Councillor in 1889. The Manor House has been owned by the council since 1912, and used as the Southall Chamber of Commerce since 1970. Situated on the east side of The Green, the building is substantially unchanged externally, compared with this earlier view.

High Street, Southall.

Southall Town Hall and Fire Station, 1904. The town hall was built in 1897, to honour
Queen Victoria's Diamond Jubilee, on land donated by the Earl of Jersey. Immediately
beyond it stands the fire station, built in 1901. This card was published just before the fire
station was enlarged. The old town hall is now a Council Customer Service Centre. The fire
station has been amalgamated with the Centre as meeting rooms internally, but externally is
unchanged from its appearance after the 1904 enlargement. The modern fire station is a little
further down the road.

Southall High Street, 1907. This view shows the enlarged fire station and, left,
W. & R. Fletcher's shop, a butcher with a second branch in West Ealing. On the right is
Edward's, draper and milliner, adorned with some flamboyant lamps. Beyond, on the corner,
stands the Three Horseshoes pub. The distant tram is on the route that reached Southall in 1901.

H.J. Butler's shop, *c.* 1914. The junction of the High Street, Broadway, South Road and Lady Margaret Road is the hub of Southall. The Broadway Buildings, left, were erected in 1905; H.J. Butler's, tailors and outfitters as well as hosiers and hatters, occupied the corner block from 1905 until the 1960s. The numbering of the buildings changed in 1928, which has led people to think Butler's moved there then, but this King & Hutchings postcard shows them *in situ* much earlier. The tram advertises Maples, another long-established local store.

Leggett's Forge, *c.* 1900. The old smithy stood at the junction of South Road and the Broadway, exactly where Butler's shop is shown above. The smithy was demolished in 1903 to make way for the 1905 buildings. The Three Horseshoes pub still exists, albeit much altered.

Above: Large crowds attending Sports Day in Southall Park, *c.* 1910. The public park was originally the gardens of Southall Park House. Sir William Ellis lived there after he retired from his post as the first Superintendant of the County Asylum (1831–38). He set up a private asylum in the house, which was later run by a Dr Boyd until the building was destroyed by fire in 1883. The tragedy led to the founding of the Southall Fire Brigade. The park was purchased by the council in 1909.

Right: The Arms of Southall–Norwood U.D.C, 1908. This card was another of those published by the Southall printer John King. It emphasizes the differences between the two sides of the borough, with the tranquil pond on Norwood Green against the relatively busy Southall High Street.

When Southall Borough Council was formed in 1936, it acquired a new coat of arms with the motto 'For All'. The use of English, rather than Latin, says much about the nature of the new borough. Southall's 1936 coat of arms can still be seen on an iron gate leading into Southall Park. In 1965 Southall was incorporated into the London Borough of Ealing.

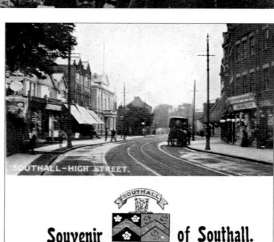

Southall station, viewed from the footbridge, in a John King postcard published *c.* 1905. The station opened in 1839, but the bridge and buildings were only erected twenty years later. It used to be an important junction when the loop line to Brentford Docks carried large quantities of freight. The prominent castellated water tower in the background, which has since been converted successfully into flats, supplied water to the gasworks, not to the railway.

A laden barge passes through Three Bridges, Southall, *c.* 1910. Windmill Lane crosses the Grand Union Canal, which in turn crosses the branch line from Southall to the Brentford Docks.

Strictly speaking, it is really only two bridges. The line took over three years to build, and this bridge was the main obstacle to overcome. It opened to goods traffic in July 1859, and was the last railway project Brunel was to see completed as he died on 30 September that year.

SOUTHALL MARKET IN 1805.

SOUTHALL MARKET, as here depicted, is of great interest from its institution, two centuries since, to the present day. In 1698, King William III. granted a charter to Francis Merrick, Esq. to hold a weekly market and two Fairs annually. In 1805, a lease was conveyed to Mr. William Welch, who laid out the sum of £1277 6s. 4d. in establishing a permanent enclosure as shown in the above picture. It became so frequented, that the old markets of Hayes and Hounslow were eventually considerably reduced in importance, and its popularity so great that it was the largest Fat Cattle Market in importance next to Smithfield. To Mr. J. Dale of the "George and Dragon" we are indebted for the privilege of reproducing this interesting old print, the original being in his possession.

PRESENT DAY.

South Road, Southall.

Above: South Road, *c.* 1930. The imposing building on the left is King's Hall Methodist church. It was built in 1916 as the King's Hall, Wesleyan Methodist chapel, designed by the architect Sir Alfred Geller of Hull, and was officially opened by Sir Charles Wakefield, Lord Mayor of London. Nowadays, on Sundays, morning services are still in English, but in the afternoon the services are held in Hindi and Urdu.

Opposite: Southall Market, 1805 and 1905. The market was (and still is) situated behind the Red Lion close to Southall Park, but has completely changed its appearance. The charter referred to in the postcard was lost for several years, but was recently found in an attic; a replica is now on permanent display in Southall Public Library.

The general market is now held on Saturdays, but horses are still auctioned on Wednesdays, and the market continues to deal in live poultry. Some 3,000 horses and ponies are sold annually, and Southall is one of only two horse fairs in the country still held every week. Trading in sheep and cattle only ceased with the foot and mouth outbreak in 2001.

Manor Parade, *c.*1906. Looking south down the road called The Green, at the junction with Osterley Park Road, Pool's Dairies occupied No. 1 on the corner, and the newsagent nearest the camera was none other than W.H. Smith. Between them lay the premises of the mysterious Madame Bull. She seems less intriguing, however, when we learn that she was Mrs Minnie Bull, draper and milliner, probably with ambitions to haute couture.

St John's church, King Street, *c.* 1908. This was the parish church of Southall, but situated at Southall Green more than 1km south of the High Street. It was built in 1838, but Southall developed so quickly that by 1910 it was too small for the enlarged congregation. The new St John's church was built nearby in Church Avenue. The old church, shown here in another of John King's 'Gazette' series, was later used as a church hall and is now a youth centre.

The Grand Union Canal at North Hyde, *c.*1900. The bridge carries the road from Norwood Green to Southall over the canal. This highly romanticised Jotter Oilette art card was published in Tuck's 'Picturesque Counties' series, but the text on the back shows considerable foresight: 'North Hyde, near Southall, is a rural spot, which as yet remains undisturbed by the ever-increasing extension of London'. The brick structure was replaced by the Wolf Bridge in 1925. The pub near the bridge is now called The Lamb. To the south along Norwood Road stands its companion pub, The Wolf.

Grand Union Canal, Southall, 1928. In the nineteenth century, the canal provided an impetus to local development. Bricks, an important local product, could now be transported cheaply and quickly into London via the Paddington Arm of the canal. This was one of the many local views published by A.L. Price, a Southall stationer.

Southall factories, 1912. T.G. Tickler Ltd, fruit growers, preservers and jam manufacturers, were a Grimsby firm who opened a second branch in Scotts Road, Southall, in 1911. T.G.'s second son, 'Bert', ran the new factory from the start, became a popular local benefactor and was a prime mover in establishing Southall-Norwood Hospital which opened in 1935. Workers can be seen enjoying a tea-break, left of the level crossing gates.

An official Otto Monsted postcard, used in 1905 to acknowledge receipt of an order. Built in 1893, opened in 1895, Otto Monsted's Works was the largest margarine factory in the country. It was situated on a private channel connected to the Grand Union Canal, had its own railway sidings and employed hundreds of local people. It was regarded as a model factory, but closed in 1929.

St Mary's church, Norwood Green, *c.* 1910. Norwood Green has had a church or chapel since the twelfth century. Re-building occurred in the fifteenth century and again in 1864 after the parish of Norwood had been established. The tower was added in 1896.

Almshouses, Frogmore Green, 1923. Built on the site of Church House (1651), the almshouses near Norwood Green were founded in 1814 by John Robins, a London cabinet maker for whom Norwood Hall was built. Note the old lady in the photograph. The message on the back says 'I shall be passing through this (Frogmore) Green presently. Norwood Green is at the far end of the pavement round the corner. I see the old woman standing outside most Sundays. She says she is a ?' (illegible). The buildings were enlarged in 1908 and were finally replaced by new almshouses in 1962.

Invitation to visit Southall, 1912. The artist of this Regent Series postcard seems to have shown remarkable foresight of events nearly half a century later!

Typical Edwardian Greetings postcard, 1911. It was published by 'F.B.' in their London Series. Even at that time, it was probably difficult to find such a rural spot 'one mile from Southall'. In the direction of Dormers Wells' perhaps?

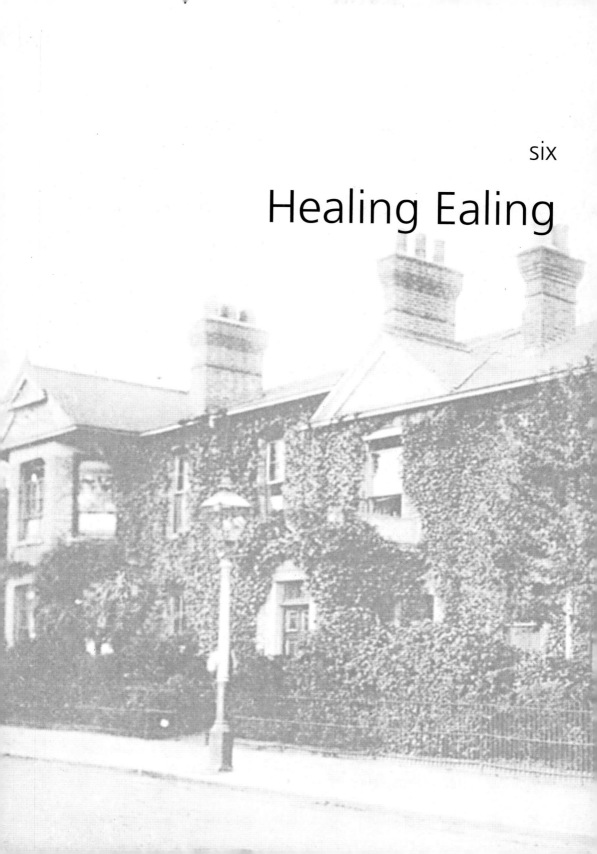

six

Healing Ealing

Above: King Edward Memorial Hospital, *c.* 1917. The hospital opened in 1911 costing £60,000, most being raised locally, supplemented by the King Edward Hospital Fund. It closed in 1979 when the new General Ealing Hospital opened. By 1985 it had been demolished and replaced by the Mattock Lane Health Centre.

The borough has always been well endowed with good hospitals. In addition to those mentioned later in this chapter, there are (or were) also Perivale Maternity and Acton Cottage Hospitals, the more recent Ealing Hospital, and St Bernard's Hospital (known as Hanwell Asylum). Opened in 1831, with a new and relatively enlightened approach, the latter housed 2,750 inmates by 1916. But how did they all originate and flourish before the days of NHS?

Until 1948, most hospitals were self-financing and had to get by in any way they could. Initial funding was often through local philanthropists and gentry, and patients who could afford it paid the going rate, but much money had to be raised from local residents, often through hospital fêtes and other sponsored events. My own memory (John Rogers) is of going into Passmore Edwards Acton Cottage Hospital, in 1943 aged 8, suffering from a broken arm and shock. No charge was made because my parents were poor, but every Christmas thereafter we received a sock made of netting so we could collect donations. This was hung religiously in a prominent place in the living room, and all visitors were expected to part with their loose change (pennies, ha'pennies and farthings). It usually amounted to a few pounds by January, and I always received a charming 'Thank you' letter from the Lady Almoner.

Opposite below: King Edward Memorial Hospital, Walter Davies Ward, *c.*1950. After service in India, Walter Davies JP MBE (1857-1946) settled in Ealing in 1913. In the First World War he was Secretary and Treasurer of the Prince of Wales Fund, responsible for the reception and housing of nearly 1,000 Belgian refugees. He was a generous patron to the hospital and St John's church, the hospital's Chairman (1921-30), President of Ealing's YMCA and Boy Scouts, and was made an Honorary Freeman of the borough in 1937.

Above: Ealing Dean Cottage Hospital, 1905. In 1871 the hospital was established in Minton Lodge, Northfield Lane (now Avenue). The wing nearest the camera housed the Frank Goodchild Memorial Ward for Children. Frank's father was a surgeon who helped to found the hospital. Frank was also a surgeon; he died tragically in 1883, aged 28, from an accidental overdose of chloroform. In 1911 the hospital was replaced by the King Edward Memorial Hospital. The Kinema Cinema (later called the Lido) was built on its site.

Above: Hanwell Cottage Hospital Grand Summer Fête, 2 August 1916 (captured in a photograph, not a postcard). Around 1,000 residents try to forget the war for an afternoon while they enjoy themselves supporting their local hospital. The Hanwell Gazette reported that the fête, held at the Grove in the grounds of Brent Valley Golf Club, was a great success even though the Countess of Jersey, who was supposed to open it, sent her apologies. Mrs Farquhar, the Rector's wife, stepped in and did the official duty. There were 132 entries for the Baby Show, another 132 (presumably different people!) played in an open-air whist drive, and a team from Cuckoo School won the relay. The sum of £95 was raised, which seems very little, but apparently was enough to get the hospital out of financial difficulties.

Hanwell Cottage Hospital was erected in Green Lane in 1900 through public subscription, as a permanent memorial of Queen Victoria's Diamond Jubilee. (Its formal name was actually the Queen Victoria and War Memorial Hospital, but locally it was known as simply 'the Cottage'.)

Voluntary subscriptions maintained it until 1948, then the NHS kept it going until 1979 when the new Ealing Hospital opened.

Opposite below: Southall-Norwood Hospital, 1965. It opened in 1935 on the corner of Osterley Park Road in a house called The Chestnuts. Bert Tickler, the jam manufacturer, was one of the benefactors, and the gasworks raised funds by charging people 6d to go up the gasometer for the view. It has since been re-named the Penny Sangam Day Hospital.

Above: St David's Home, Castlebar Hill, *c.* 1950. This stands on the site of Castle Hill Lodge, once owned by Edward, Duke of Kent, who was Queen Victoria's father. That house was demolished around 1830 and was replaced by Kent House, built in the 1840s. Henry de Bruno Austin, the man who went bankrupt trying to develop the area, lived there for a time. In 1918 it became St David's Home for disabled ex-servicemen. Considerably rebuilt and extended, with a chapel added in 1919, it continues to serve the same function today.

Military Hospital, Southall, *c*. 1918. This was actually the Maypole Institute, built in 1910 as a social club for Otto Monsted's margarine factory employees. It became a temporary military hospital during the First World War, but now serves as Southall's Community Centre. The message on the back, written by a patient, reads: 'This is a small military hospital at Southall. It only holds 100 beds. It is an English hospital. It is managed by voluntary aid ladies and is rather nice'.

St Marylebone School, 1915. Opened in November 1858, on the west side of South Road, Southall, the school maintained 424 poor children at the expense of the ratepayers of the Parish of Marylebone. At the time this postcard was published, the building was used as a hospital for wounded Australian soldiers. After the war, it became St Joseph's Roman Catholic School for girls. It was eventually sold in 1931 and demolished in 1934.